A STUDENT'S GUIDE TO ESTATES IN LAND AND FUTURE INTERESTS:

Text, Examples, Problems and Answers

Second Edition

Robert Laurence
Professor of Law
University of Arkansas

Pamela B. Minzner
Judge, New Mexico Court of Appeals

Graphics by:

Carolyn E. Kennedy
Paralegal
Freedman, Boyd, Daniels, Peifer,
Hollander, Guttmann & Goldberg, P.A.
Albuquerque

STUDENT GUIDE SERIES

1993

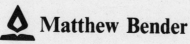 Matthew Bender

 Times Mirror
Books

Library of Congress Cataloging-in-Publication Data

Laurence, Robert, 1945-
    A students's guide to estates in land and future interests : text,
examples, problems, and answers / Robert Laurence, Pamela B.
Minzner. -- 2nd ed.
        p.   cm. -- (Student guide series)
    ISBN 0-256-15031-1
    1. Future interests--United States--Outlines, syllabi, etc.
2. Estates (Law)--United States--Outlines, syllabi, etc.
I. Minzner, Pamela B. II. Title. III. Series.
KF605.L385   1993
346.7304'2--dc20
[347.30642]
                                                        93-14440
                                                            CIP

MATTHEW BENDER & CO., INC.
EDITORIAL OFFICES
11 PENN PLAZA, NEW YORK, NY 10001–2006 (212) 967-7707
2101 WEBSTER STREET, OAKLAND, CA 94612–3027 (510) 446-7700

(Matthew Bender & Co., Inc.)   (Pub. 635)

For Frederick M. Hart
Our teacher, colleague, and friend

PREFACE TO THE SECOND EDITION

The first edition of *A Student's Guide to Estates in Land and Future Interests* was successful in ways surprising to many, not least to the authors. Many thousands of students during the '80s and early '90s turned to it to guide them through what is—or can be—one of the dreary parts of the Property course, a worm in the otherwise savory apple of the first year of law school. While we are hesitant to say that the *Student's Guide* made the going either easy or pleasant, it seems to have made the learning palatable and the experience tolerable, which is about all we ever aimed for anyway.

Students may be interested to know of the origins of this book. In a very real way it began on the floor of the living room of Anne Kass, now a trial judge in New Mexico, as Laurence and his study group struggled to prepare for Minzner's exam. Feeling ourselves to be the latest in the long line of generations of American law students trying to figure out what an executory interest was, we started drawing diagrams and making charts, and things began to fall into place, we hoped. Well, we made it, and you will too.

From those early sketches, the presentation was formalized and tried out on patient students at the University of New Mexico and, later, at the University of North Dakota. It seemed to work, and Matthew Bender & Co. took a chance on the book, its unknown authors and its unusual format. The book did well and became the first in a series of "Student Guides" from Matthew Bender.

The *Student's Guide* never was a treatise requiring careful updating. Rather, it's a teaching book, and we've discovered over the years some pedagogic changes that we think should be made. But, we admit, the changes are relatively few. The original *Student's Guide to Estates in Land and Future Interests* has been too successful and well received by students to make us eager to make many changes, and we hope that you can still see on each page the imprint of a student like yourself trying to learn a strange and difficult subject.

Nevertheless, technology has caught up with us. The original diagrams were painstakingly drawn by hand by Carol Kennedy; the same artist has drawn them here while sitting at a computer terminal. We hope you approve of the change.

One final point, one perhaps addressed to the teachers rather than the students: over the past decade, we have become more and more certain that the distinction that more than anything causes students difficulty is the one between the contingent remainder and the executory interest. In a large measure, the approach of the book, with the constant emphasis on the year 1536, is aimed to make that distinction understandable. We note here that we write in the present tense as much as possible. We describe a system of estates in land that never really existed in fact. Later in the presentation we modify the system by statute so that it becomes the modern law of estates in land. We use the present tense to describe this artificially simplified system so students will not be tempted to ask when? in what order? which came first?

It is appropriate here to include the acknowledgment of help that was in the First Edition: These materials are the product of a number of people, not all of whom appear on the title page. Ms. Lynn Cianci Eby, New Mexico '78, put together an original outline, problem set, and answers from which Chapter Seven and Appendix II heavily draw. Ms. Alice E. Herter, New Mexico '79, developed a series of slide presentations which improved the original presentation and influenced the textual treatment in this manuscript. Claudette Abel, Cory Carlson, Richard Gleason and Karen Johnson, all North Dakota '81, provided valuable assistance researching the property law of the several states. Ms. Johnson deserves special mention for her efficient and professional direction of the editorial process. Ms. Adele Hunter, formerly of the University of New Mexico School of Law staff, typed all of the drafts.

Since the original appearance of this *Student's Guide*, we have had valuable advice given by many, many people. Of course, much of that advice came from our students who used the text with varying degrees of enthusiasm. Also, our colleagues at the New Mexico, North Dakota, Arkansas and Florida State law schools, as well as teachers from around the country, helped us improve the presentation. These persons are too numerous to be named here, but we thank them all, even while admitting that we didn't always follow their advice.

Robert Laurence   Pamela B. Minzner
Fayetteville   Albuquerque

January 1993

PREFACE

The American legal system belongs to the common law family of legal systems. Although the American colonies might have chosen otherwise, the private law choice in favor of receiving English common law was made in the early life of each of the various American states other than Louisiana. The significance of the election to receive English common law, of course, has lessened with the modern emphasis on legislative innovation and in particular with such important legislative events as the Uniform Commercial Code and the Uniform Probate Code.

Nevertheless, the English common law experience remains, even in the twentieth century, the most important reason for that particular—some would say peculiar—set of concepts and a good deal of vocabulary we call the law of real property. A traditional introduction to the law of real property has been a sketchy survey of the period between 1066 and 1290, from which a good bit of the intellectual heritage may flow. It was during this period, for example, that the concepts of alienability by gift or sale and inheritability by intestate succession appear to have become associated with an individual's interests in real property. It was during this period, further, that a range of interests in land of a rather different sort was recognized. It became possible, perhaps incidentally, to acquire and hold interests measured in terms of time, for one's life for example, or for the life of one's bloodline as represented by direct descendants, and for other periods.

The era from 1066 to 1290 saw the institution of Norman feudalism in England and the emergence of a property system which proved better and stronger than its feudal beginnings. It is not at all clear that the so-called English common law system of estates in land, which evolved as the English common law itself emerged, was a direct or necessary result of the feudal times which fostered both. It does seem clear, however, that the English common law system of estates and associated doctrines were at least an indirect result of the economic aspects of the feudalism which William the Conqueror introduced and strengthened in the aftermath of 1066.

The property law that emerged in the English feudal era seems to have been a reasonable response to contemporary social and economic conditions. More important, however, that same set of feudal ideas still seems to provide a useful body of Property law, even today. In this book, in order to emphasize the practical significance of English real property law, we have de-emphasized English legal history.

We have tried to isolate those concepts which are basic for the beginning American law student and to clarify the relationship those concepts have to each other. A relatively coherent, conceptual system can be extracted from the English common law of real property. We offer that system as an effective introduction for beginning law students.

This book is not a treatise in the ordinary sense of the word. That is not to say that we have not given it a great deal of thought; we have. But this is not a scholarly treatment of the law of estates in land. That has been done, often and well. *See* T. Bergin & P. Haskell, *Preface to Estates in Land & Future Interests* (2d ed. 1984); J. Cribbett, *Principles of the Law of Property* (2d ed. 1975); C. Moynihan, *Introduction to the Law of Real Property* (1962); R. Powell, *Real Property*. This book is a learning tool: a presentation of the material covered in a first-year property course in a way which makes sense to us and has made sense to our students.

We believe our presentation is special in three ways. First, the text will introduce you, in a formalistic, even mechanistic, and certainly oversimplified form, to a system of estates in land that never existed. History has taken second place to logic, detail to broad outline, and practical importance to a chronological presentation. We have found that such a presentation provides a firm base on which other discussions of the topic may build. Furthermore, we think it is possible that other approaches obscure the essential legacy of English common law and equity: a set of concepts and a technical vocabulary to express those concepts.

This book is unique in a second way, we think. The presentation is a series of symbolic representations of the various interests in real property. These symbols are intended to make the sometimes slippery distinction among the various interests less slippery, although we decline to say "easy to grasp." The development of the symbols into their present form and completeness is ours, but their origins are elsewhere. Persons familiar with J. Dukeminier & S. Johanson, *Family Wealth Transactions: Wills, Trusts, Future Interests and Estate Planning* (1972), will recognize the germinal nature of the work and the debt we cheerfully acknowledge. Also, the geometric properties of the system will be obvious and, hence, some credit must go to patient high school students in DeWitt, New York; Andover, Massachusetts; and Moriarty, New Mexico. The use of graphics to make abstract ideas more comprehensible is certainly far older than we are, but it is interesting that relatively little use is made of such techniques in law teaching or, for that matter, in judicial opinions. *But cf. State v. Unterscher*, 289 N.W.2d 201 (N.D. 1980). The presentation that follows offers graphical examples and encourages the use of such diagrams by students in independent study.

Finally, the presentation includes extensive problem sets, with answers and explanations. The problems have been answered as they would have been at English common law (fixed somewhat arbitrarily as of 1700) and at the end of the presentation as they would be affected by statutes such as those included in Appendix III, representing in 1993 the states of California, Illinois, Minnesota, New Mexico, and North Dakota. We hope you will find your state or a state with a statute similar to yours in that list. If not, you are invited to learn the common law and the analysis necessary to solve the problems in your state.

We begin, then, with the definition of five present, possessory estates in real property and how they are created.

TABLE OF CONTENTS

CHAPTER THREE

THE FAMILY OF REMAINDERS

CHAPTER FOUR

PRESENT AND FUTURE INTERESTS AFTER 1536

CHAPTER FIVE

LATER MODIFICATIONS OF THE
BASIC COMMON LAW SCHEME:
Common Law Responses to the Statute of Uses

CHAPTER SIX

A FEW INTERESTING COMPLEXITIES

CHAPTER SEVEN

STATUTORY MODIFICATIONS

Page

CHAPTER ONE

THE BASIC PRESENT, POSSESSORY ESTATES

A. Blackacre

Observe the estate of Blackacre, the traditional metaphor for an interest in real property:

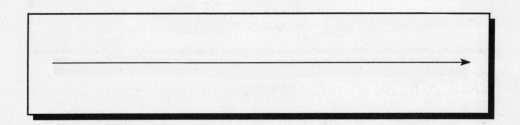

That's right. For the purposes of this presentation, we describe neither green hills, gurgling streams, nor quietly lowing cows or honking geese. Strong-backed farmers working the field, stately baronial mansions, and stone and rail fences older than memory are not provided for color. We ask that you consider merely a ray, a graphical representation of the traditional metaphor.

Yet much symbolism is tied up in that ray. For one thing, the arrow represents infinitely long duration; the arrow represents endlessness of the time dimension. The ray also suggests, by representing time as a continuous phenomenon, that interests in Blackacre may be divided between present and future interests. Indeed they may. More, much more, will be said later of this particular legacy from the English law of property.

We might also take one quick cross-sectional look at the ray representing Blackacre:

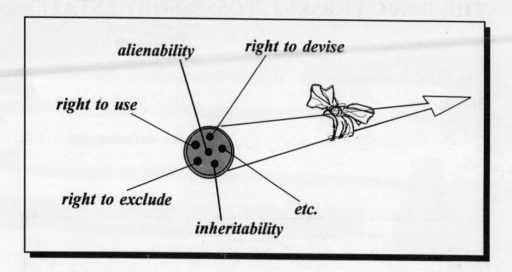

Voilá! A bundle of rights. We leave to your property course a closer inspection of each of these rights and the limitations on them. Some of these aspects of English property law duplicate or parallel concepts found in the property law of civil law countries. The time or durational dimension, however, appears to be unique to the property law of the common law countries, and we principally focus on that dimension. Our task is to illustrate the ways in which Blackacre can be divided among those whose rights are present rights to present possession and those whose rights are present rights to future possession. This possibility of division between present and future interests is a special legacy of the English common law system of estates. Hence, again, Blackacre:

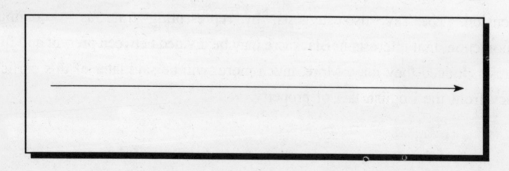

B.   Four Present, Possessory Estates

English common law lawyers developed a few basic ways in which present, possessory rights in Blackacre might be owned. Here are four of them, with their corresponding symbols:

1.   The Fee Simple Absolute, a/k/a/ Fee Simple or Fee

X is said to own a *Fee Simple Absolute* interest in Blackacre if:

(a)   X is entitled to the present possession of Blackacre;

(b)   X is entitled to the future possession of Blackacre until X dies;

(c)   X's heir, as determined by the Canons of Descent, is entitled to possession of Blackacre immediately upon X's death;

> *The principal Canon of Descent was that persons of closer consanguinity to X took the property over those of more distant relationship. When two persons had equal relationship to the deceased owner of Blackacre (1) males took over females and (2) the elder male took over the younger male. Females shared equally if there were no males. With the exception of this last rule, the descent of the British Crown is governed by the Canons. Few other things are governed by the Canons of Descent, as there has been rather sweeping statutory reformation.*

(d)   the heir of X's heir, as likewise determined, is entitled to the possession of Blackacre immediately upon the death of X's heir;

(e)   and so on, through an indefinite succession of heirs; and

(f)   notwithstanding (c), (d) and (e), X or anyone who inherited Blackacre from X or X's heirs may, at any time and without the consent of anyone who might later inherit Blackacre, alienate all or part of Blackacre through the use of any of the grants described below.

We will symbolize X's fee simple absolute as:

X's fee simple absolute ⟶

The fee simple absolute is the most complete form of ownership recognized at common law, and the symbol is intended to reflect that there are no conditions on possession, inheritance, or survivorship. The fee simple continues forever. Is it absolute ownership? No. Don't forget the "power" dimension: it may still be illegal to build a rendering plant outside your neighbor's breakfast nook. What we mean by "most complete" will become clearer as we look at less complete ownership, but a few characteristics may be mentioned here:

a.   Possession of Blackacre is conditioned only by the restrictions that society legitimately places upon private property rights. *See State v. Shack*, 58 N.J. 297, 277 A.2d 369 (1971), or *Reid v. Architectural Board*, 119 Ohio App. 67, 192 N.E.2d 74 (1963), for examples of such restrictions.

b.   The estate in fee simple is indefinitely inheritable. At classic common law, inheritance reflected the principle of

Primogeniture (the second Canon of Descent was called the Rule of Primogeniture); the inheritance rules were complex, male-dominated and yet were functional. The system tended to send property to one person rather than divide it up among several heirs. Today, statutes, which vary to some extent from state to state, dictate how property is transferred at death. Some statutes govern an owner's right to dispose of property by a written document called a "will"; such statutes permit land to be "devised." Other statutes dictate the persons who succeed to the property of a person who dies without a will; under these statutes, land would be "inherited" by "heirs." In these materials, we use the word "devisable" to describe the right to leave property by will and the word "inheritable" to describe the right to have one's "heirs" take one's property absent a will.

c. A fee simple is freely alienable inter vivos. This means that it can be sold or given away by its owner.

The fee simple might be illustrated graphically once more for emphasis:

X's Fee Simple Absolute ⟶

1. Alienable
2. Inheritable
3. Devisable, after the Statute of Wills (1540)

2. **Fee Tail (from "tailler", Norman French for "to cut" or "to carve"); Entailed Estate**

X is said to own a Fee Tail interest in Blackacre if:

(a)   X is entitled to the present possession of Blackacre;

(b)   X is entitled to the future possession of Blackacre until X's death;

(c)   upon X's death, only X's children are entitled to inherit (among the children, the Canons of Descent apply);

(d)   upon the death of X's child who inherited from X, the children of X's child who inherited from X are entitled to inherit;

(e)   and so on, through an indefinite succession of lineal heirs of X [*"lineal heirs" are sons, daughters, grandchildren, great-grandchildren; cousins, nieces, nephews, uncles, aunts are called "collateral heirs"*]; and, finally,

(f)   X or any of X's lineal heirs who inherit Blackacre may alienate only his or her right to possession of Blackacre until death. At the time of such death, regardless of who is in possession of Blackacre, the estate passes to X's lineal heir, as described above.

Since the fee tail will pass only to the lineal heirs of X, there may come a time at which no one is eligible to own Blackacre—when X's direct line dies out. This event we call "*Expiration*," denoted in the diagram by *Ex*. You should be aware that most writers and courts do not use this word as narrowly as we do. When you see the word in this book, it means the natural termination of the fee tail or the life estate.

You should also note that a fee simple does *not* expire. While X's direct line may die out, theoretically, at least, we should always be able to find an heir of X.

> *The fee tail probably was the most significant estate planning device in the years between 1285 and 1472. In 1472 a technique called "common recovery" was sanctioned, which allowed the interests of the lineal heirs to be frustrated. The details of this remedy are beyond the scope of this presentation, but the popularity of the fee tail and its eventual demise are evidence of the relationship between social history and the evolution of legal concepts.*

A few characteristics of the fee tail:

a.   As with the fee simple, possession of Blackacre is without condition, other than those restrictions that society might place upon private property rights.

b.   Blackacre is inheritable only by the direct lineal descendants of the original owner.

c.   Blackacre is not freely alienable. The only thing that any owner may alienate is the right to possession for the life of that owner; on the owner's death the property passes automatically to that owner's direct lineal heir.

The fee tail might be illustrated once more for emphasis:

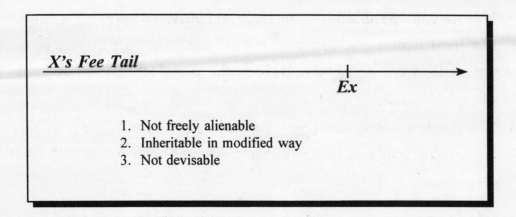

X's Fee Tail

Ex

1. Not freely alienable
2. Inheritable in modified way
3. Not devisable

Note the words given above: "The only thing that any owner may alienate is the right to possession for that owner's lifetime." Does your new-to-the-law mind rebel just a bit at the notion that there is *more* to the ownership of property than the right to possess it during one's lifetime? It is important to your understanding of estates in land and especially future interests that you accept the notion that full ownership of property is much more than a lifetime's worth of possessory rights. The land will still be there after the owner dies, and the full ownership of the property during life includes the right to specify its disposition upon death. Thus, you see the major difference between the fee simple and the fee tail. The fee simple owner controls disposition; the fee tail owner does not—his or her children are guaranteed possession irrespective of their parent's desires.

In the next estate, the life estate, the owner has no control over the property's disposition at death and his or her children are *not* entitled to possession.

3. Life Estate; Estate for Life

X is said to own a *Life Estate* interest in Blackacre if:

(a)   X is entitled to the present possession of Blackacre,

(b) X is entitled to the future possession of Blackacre until X's death,

(c) X's heirs are entitled to inherit nothing by way of X's ownership of Blackacre, and

(d) X may alienate only the right to possession of Blackacre during X's life.

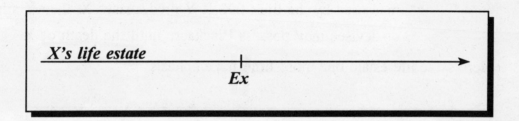

Here, expiration is upon X's death.

a. Possession is without condition; but, remember, possession is only of the life estate. The life tenant has no right to possess something belonging to a future tenant. This limitation presents some problems. For example, how can a life tenant enjoy a heavily wooded Blackacre if he or she wants to build a factory and the future tenant is an ardent environmentalist? The problem of balancing the interests of a life tenant and a future tenant was resolved at English common law by the doctrine of waste. The doctrine of waste limits the life tenant's use of the land, but the doctrine is flexible and permits a court to balance the competing interests. Thus, we characterize the life estate, as well as the fee tail, as an unconditional possessory interest.

b. The life estate is not inheritable. It expires with X, leaving nothing for X's heirs to inherit.

c.   The life estate is freely alienable, but expiration still occurs on X's death. If X sells to Y, Y holds a life estate that expires on X's death, a so-called life estate *pur autre vie* ("for the life of another"). This modification of the basic life estate is not essentially different from the basic form, except that a life estate *pur autre vie* is inheritable and can be devised. For example, if X sells to Y, Y has an interest in Blackacre measured by the life of X. If Y predeceases X, then Y's heir or devisee may possess Blackacre until the death of X.

Here's the life estate one more time for emphasis:

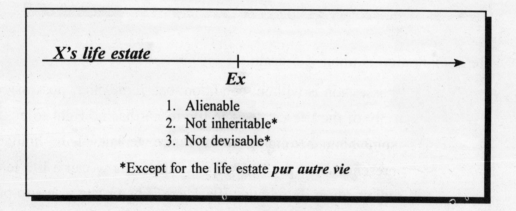

X's life estate

Ex

1. Alienable
2. Not inheritable*
3. Not devisable*

*Except for the life estate *pur autre vie*

4. Fee Simple Determinable, Determinable Fee

X is said to own a *Fee Simple Determinable* interest in Blackacre if:

(a)   X is entitled to the present possession of Blackacre;

(b)   X is entitled to the future possession of Blackacre until his death;

(c)   X's heir, as determined by the Canons of Descent, is entitled to possession of Blackacre immediately upon X's death;

(d)   the heir of X's heir, as likewise determined, is entitled to the possession of Blackacre immediately upon the death of the person from whom he inherited;

(e)   and so on, through an indefinite succession of heirs; and

(f)   notwithstanding (c), (d) and (e), X or anyone who inherited Blackacre from X or X's heirs may, at any time and without the consent of anyone who might later inherit Blackacre, alienate all or part of Blackacre through the use of any of the grants described below.

exactly as in the definition of a fee simple absolute, *subject to* a self-executing condition that, if broken, removes the possession of Blackacre from X.

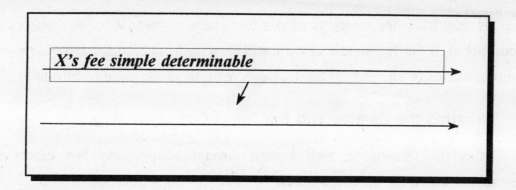

X's fee simple determinable

The fee simple determinable, you will note, does not expire.

a.   Possession is conditional, however. Blackacre may always have to be farmed, for example, or always used for church purposes, depending on the condition.

b.   Blackacre is indefinitely inheritable.

c.   Blackacre is freely alienable.

d.   Blackacre is devisable, after the Statute of Wills (1540).

(b) and (d) ought not surprise you, because this estate, as the name suggests, is a type of *fee simple*.

The fee simple determinable was not nearly so important at English common law as the first three estates you learned. It is possible that the estate served at an early time as a device to secure the repayment of a loan; *i.e.*, a mortgage. For example, early forms of mortgages may have resembled conditional conveyances; O might convey to his creditor as long as a sum of money remained owed to that creditor. There appears to have been a low incidence of use of the fee simple determinable in England; however, in this country the fee simple determinable occurred with greater frequency. It has been used in conveyances to charities, in conveyances that restrict land use, and in conveyances to railroads for rights-of-way.

There is a fifth present, possessory interest that might be introduced now, the fee simple on condition subsequent, but we will get to that shortly. This fifth interest will be easier to grasp if we introduce some other ideas first. Some questions may have been nagging at you for a page or two: Who says possession is conditional in the fee simple determinable? Who limits the fee tail? How does X know what he or she has? Who decides? We turn to the creation of the estates.

C. Creating the Estates and the Art of Conveyancing

Meet the famous O, well known throughout property law casebooks. Suppose O owns a fee simple absolute.

> *An early eastern religion pictured the world supported on the backs of three elephants. The elephants stood on the backs of two turtles. It is improper to ask upon what the turtles stood.*

O may create a fee simple absolute in A with the following grant:

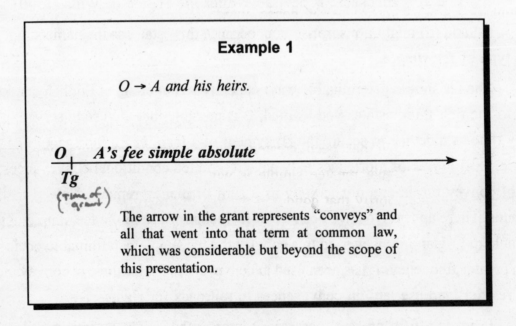

Example 1

O → A and his heirs.

O   *A's fee simple absolute* ⟶
| Tg
(Time of grant)

The arrow in the grant represents "conveys" and all that went into that term at common law, which was considerable but beyond the scope of this presentation.

The common law was very specific about how to create a fee simple absolute. These words, ***and no others***, would do.

You can see that O owns Blackacre until the time of the grant (*Tg*), at which point A takes over. Thereafter, A's interest in Blackacre is as complete as the law recognizes. The entire time dimension is occupied by A's interest; no one else has an interest in the property.

What about A's heirs? The conveyance was, after all, "to A and his heirs." While A is alive, A's heirs are unidentifiable. A person's heir is determined on his death—a living person has no heirs, only potential heirs. Under the Canons of Descent, A's eldest son has the most likely chance of inheritance but the eldest son won't be A's heir unless he's still living at A's death. But, even if A has no *close* relatives, that doesn't mean he won't have an heir when he dies. A complete stranger, for example a distant cousin in another county, might in fact become A's heir. If A and all of A's direct descendants die in a common accident, for example, a collateral heir would inherit under the Canons of Descent. So, *no* living person has an heir, but *every* deceased person does.

It was decided early at common law that the words "and his heirs" gave nothing to A's heirs and were not, hence, words of purchase. The only word that describes the recipient, and thus the only word of purchase in the grant "to A and his heirs," is the word "A." A is the "purchaser," which meant to the common law lawyers that A had either been given or had bought the land.

The words "and his heirs" are words of limitation; that is to say, they indicate the estate that has been created, the fee simple absolute. We know, practically speaking, that the fee simple is without limitation. You'll see some words of limitation shortly that condition the use of the estate A has been given. The point here is that words of limitation "limit," or describe, the grantee's estate, but do not give rights in the estate to anyone other than A.

O may grant a fee tail to A with the following conveyance:

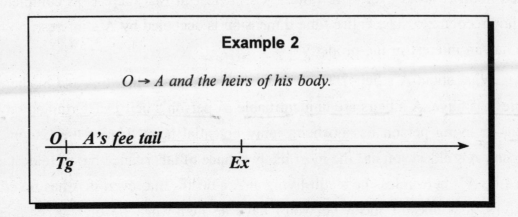

Notice that the entire time dimension of Blackacre has not been accounted for. We have, as yet, no ownership assigned to the time beyond expiration; that is, the time after A's direct line runs out. Be patient; we will take care of this "future interest" in good time.

In this grant, "A" is the word of purchase and "and the heirs of his body" are the words of limitation. These latter words limit the estate that A receives. We will not know which heir of A's body (that is, which of his or her children) will inherit until A dies. Therefore no one takes anything at the time of the grant except A. Just as in the fee simple absolute, there are no words of purchase except "A" in the grant.

There are some special forms of the fee tail:

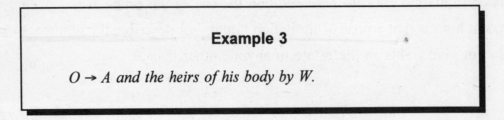

This grant creates a "fee tail special," and only children of both A and W are eligible to inherit.

1) Fee tail Special
2) Fee tail Male
3) Fee tail Female

> ### Examples 4 and 5
>
> *O → A and the male heirs of his body.*
>
> *O → A and the female heirs of his body.*

These are the "fee tail male" and "fee tail female"; they are self-explanatory. Apparently, no one ever thought to try:

> ### Example 6
>
> *O → A and the basketball-playing heirs of his body.*

However, it's hard to believe that no one tried:

> ### Example 7
>
> *O → A and the Harvard-educated heirs of his body.*

In any case, we recognize only the basic fee tail and the three special forms first discussed.

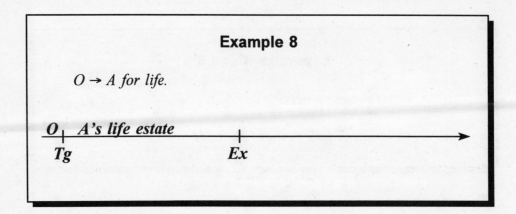

Example 8

$O \rightarrow A$ *for life.*

O   A's life estate
Tg   Ex

The life estate is the preferred estate at the common law; that is, the law presumed that a life estate was created by any grant that did not fit one of the other estates. As Littleton wrote late in the fifteenth century: "For a man purchase lands by the words, 'To have and to hold to him for ever' ... he hath but an estate for term of life, for that there lack these words, 'his heirs', which words only make an estate of inheritance in all feoffments and grants." *Littleton's Tenures* § 1 (Wambaugh ed., 1903).

This preference has now been generally abandoned, by statute, but we will retain it here as part of our simplified system. We will tinker with the system later.

Thus, the following examples all create life estates in A:

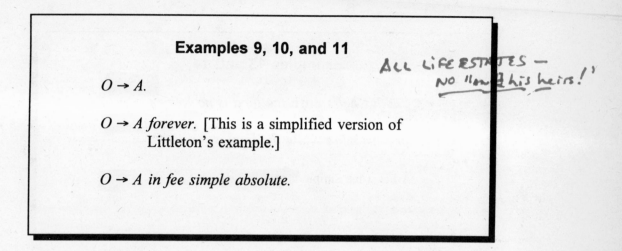

Examples 9, 10, and 11

O → A.

O → A forever. [This is a simplified version of
Littleton's example.]

O → A in fee simple absolute.

[handwritten: ALL LIFE ESTATES — No "and his heirs!"]

Why? No words of limitation are present that the common law recognized
as creating anything other than a life estate. No "and his heirs." No "and the heirs
of his body."

Finally, O may grant a fee simple determinable to A:

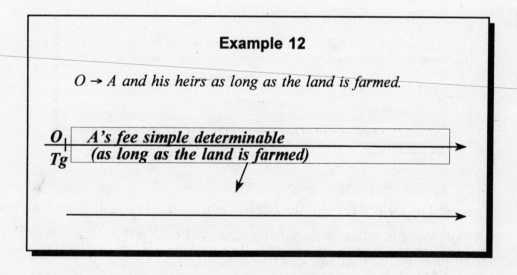

Example 12

O → A and his heirs as long as the land is farmed.

$\dfrac{O}{Tg}$ | *A's fee simple determinable
(as long as the land is farmed)*

The common law was not so strict on the wording of this grant, although
the words "and his heirs" were still required.

Examples 13 and 14

O → A and his heirs **until** *the land is no longer farmed.*

O → A and his heirs **while** *the land is farmed.*

A has a fee simple determinable.

Here, of course, we have used one condition: that the land be farmed. Any, or almost any, condition will do; O decides. There will of course be public policy limitations on what conditions will be enforceable.

Sometimes statutes reflect public policy limitations; sometimes courts announce limitations when called upon to interpret or construe deeds or wills. As you might expect, statutes and decided cases are easier to take into account in drafting documents than issues that have never been litigated.

The symbol for the fee simple determinable indicates that if the land is not farmed A will lose his estate and someone else will take possession. "Who?" you ask. This "future interest" will be discussed shortly.

There is one other present, possessory interest that we promised to discuss: the fee simple on condition subsequent.

X is said to own a *Fee Simple on Condition Subsequent* interest in Blackacre if:

(a) X is entitled to the present possession of Blackacre;

(b) X is entitled to the future possession of Blackacre until his death;

(c) X's heir, as determined by the Canons of Descent, is entitled to possession of Blackacre immediately upon X's death;

(d) the heir of X's heir, as likewise determined, is entitled to the possession of Blackacre immediately upon the death of the person from whom he inherited;

(e) and so on, through an indefinite succession of heirs; and

} exactly as in the definition of a fee simple absolute, *subject to* a condition that, if broken, allows the creator of the estate (the grantor) to enter the land and reclaim it. This right to enter and reclaim is passed from the grantor to his or her heirs, and the original grantor need not be alive when the condition is broken. However, for simplicity, we will say that the grantor may enter when we mean the grantor or those who succeed the grantor at death. *NOTE: Until 1536 this right could not be sold or given to a third party.*

(f) notwithstanding (c), (d) and (e), X or anyone who inherited Blackacre from X or X's heirs may, at any time and without the consent of anyone who might later inherit Blackacre, alienate all or part of Blackacre through the use of any of the grants described below.

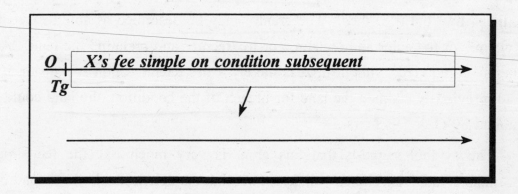

The conveyance that creates a fee simple on condition subsequent:

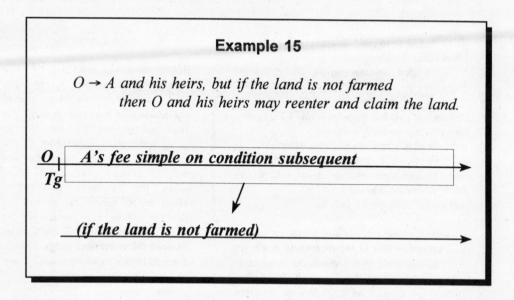

Example 15

*O → A and his heirs, but if the land is not farmed
then O and his heirs may reenter and claim the land.*

A's fee simple on condition subsequent

(if the land is not farmed)

Once again, as with the fee simple determinable, other wordings are acceptable. You may substitute "provided that if ... then" or "on the condition that if ... then" for "but if ... then." The grantor may be described as able to "reenter and claim," or to "enter and reclaim," or to "reenter and reclaim" the land. "And his heirs" is required; without it, A is merely a life tenant. Upon A's death, if O has not previously claimed the land for breach of the condition, the land could be reclaimed by O or O's heirs.

The symbol suggests that this grant is very much like the fee simple determinable, and it is. The only difference is that the determinable fee's condition is self-executing, while that in the fee simple on condition subsequent requires O to enter and reclaim Blackacre. Who cares? Well, at least theoretically, a statute of limitations might operate differently in the case of an optional right and in the case of a self-executing condition.

The question of the application of a statute of limitations ties in, of course, with your study of rights acquired by adverse possession. The requisite period of possession is measured from the time a cause of action in ejectment accrues. When

automatic ejectment

O has created a fee simple determinable, one could argue that O's cause of action accrues the moment when the condition is broken, thereby giving O the immediate right to possession. Hence, the statute of limitations governing ejectment would begin to run automatically when the condition was broken.

However, when O creates a fee simple on condition subsequent, then he is not entitled to possession until he demands it. One might argue that only after demand and refusal does O have a cause of action in ejectment, and only then does the statute of limitations begin to run.

> *Of course, a legislature might choose to restrict the period of time during which O might validly make such a demand. In other words, there may be specific statutory provisions governing the exercise of an optional right. Furthermore, the statutes might treat the optional right in the same manner as the self-executing condition. Finally, a court of equity might well apply the doctrine of laches to a long-unexercised right of entry.*

These, then, are five basic present, possessory estates in land. Master them; it will be important that you be able to classify a present estate with a glance at a conveyance. Otherwise, what follows will become unmanageable. There will be, however, only one more present, possessory estate to master.

D.   Review Problem Set (in the year 1500)

[We feel compelled to date these problems because of events in 1536 that will be described later. For those of you working through this book for the first time, the date may be ignored. Answer the problems using what you know now.]

1.   O wants to give his land to his only child, but O wants to make sure the land will stay in the family forever. How should he proceed?

> Fee Tail
>
> O to A and the heirs of his body.

2.   O wants to sell her property for the highest possible price. How should she proceed?

> Fee Simple Absolute
>
> O to A and his heirs

3.   O wants to give his land to A, but he never wants the land to be used for commercial purposes. Can he do so? How?

> Either Fee Simple Determinable; Fee Simple Condition Subsequent
> O To A and his heirs for As long as the land is never used for commercial purposes
> O to A and his heirs But if the land is used for commercial purposes, then
> to O and his heirs' to reenter and reclaim the land

4.   O wants to give her land to the Unitarian Church as long as it is used for church purposes, but if it ceases to be used for church purposes, O wants to be able to take back the property. Can she do so? How?

and its assigns

> Same as above
> O to Unitarian Church and its assigns for as long as it is used for church purposes.
> O to Unitarian Church and it assigns on the condition that if the property ceases to be used to church purposes then to O and its heirs the right to reenter and reclaim the land

5.   O wants to give her land to her husband until he dies. Can she do so? How?

> O to A for life
> O to A
> O to A forever
>
> Assumption

Answers to Review Problem Set

1. O wants to give his land to his only child, but O wants to make sure the land will stay in the family forever. How should he proceed?

    He should create a fee tail:

    O → Child and the heirs of his body.

2. O wants to sell her property for the highest possible price. How should she proceed?

    She should create a fee simple absolute:

    O → Purchaser and his heirs.

3. O wants to give his land to A, but he never wants the land to be used for commercial purposes. Can he do so? Yes. How?

    He might create a fee simple determinable:

    O → A and his heirs as long as the land is never used for commercial purposes.

    Or, he might create a fee simple on condition subsequent:

    O → A and his heirs, but if the land is ever used for commercial purposes, then O and his heirs shall have the right to reenter and reclaim the land.

    The fee simple determinable and the fee simple on condition subsequent are not interchangeable methods of conveying property. Your client's wishes, governing statutes and controlling cases will be relevant.

4.   O wants to give her land to the Unitarian Church as long as it is used for church purposes, but if it ceases to be used for church purposes, O wants to be able to take back the property. Can she do so? Yes. How?

She may do so by creating a fee simple subject to condition subsequent:

O → The Unitarian Church, its successors and assigns, but if the land ceases to be used for church purposes, O or her heirs may reenter and reclaim the land.

> *The Church has no "heirs." With corporate entities, use the words "its successors and assigns" instead.*

5.   O wants to give her land to her husband until he dies. Can she do so? Yes. How?

She may do so by simply creating a life estate:

O → Husband for life.

CHAPTER TWO

FUTURE INTERESTS BEFORE 1536

You have seen enough representations on the diagrams in Chapter One of what are called "future interests": the missing pieces in the diagrams following the expiration of the life estate or the fee tail, or following the breaking of the condition in the fee simple determinable or fee simple on condition subsequent. These as-yet unassigned parts of Blackacre are not, of course, physical "parts" of the land, but rather they are interests that are in some sense future. They are *future* interests in the sense that they will not become *possessory* interests, if ever, until some future time. But you know from your property course that "ownership" of property does not require its possession. The "future interests" are presently protected property rights, only the possession of which has been delayed.

The first category, and the easiest to master, identifies future interests retained by the grantor, O.

A. Future Interests in the Grantor

Throughout this text, we will assume O owns a fee simple absolute unless the discussion or the problem indicates otherwise. Thus, when O conveys to A a fee simple absolute, O grants A that which O owns: no future interest is created; O retains no interest in Blackacre.

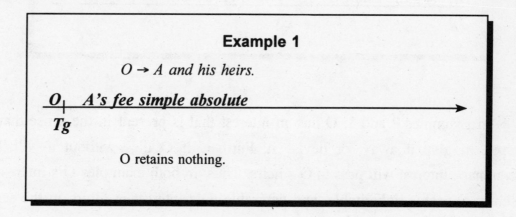

Example 1

$O \rightarrow A$ and his heirs.

$\underline{O}$ *A's fee simple absolute* $\longrightarrow$
Tg

O retains nothing.

25

In the case of each of the other four present estates we have discussed, the common law determined that, with no further words than the grants you have already seen, O retains the future interest. O, in other words, owns a present right to future possession of the land. Your major task is to learn the vocabulary.

With two of the four present estates, if O says nothing further, O retains the future interest known as a reversion.

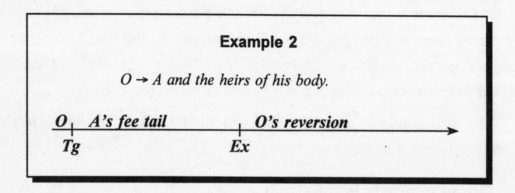

Example 2

$O \rightarrow A$ *and the heirs of his body.*

O | A's fee tail | O's reversion
Tg | | Ex

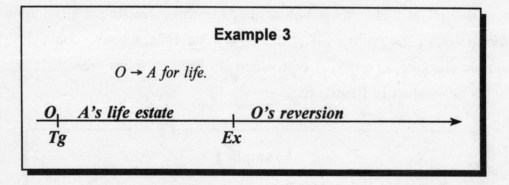

Example 3

$O \rightarrow A$ *for life.*

O | A's life estate | O's reversion
Tg | | Ex

In Examples 2 and 3, O has an interest that is present in the sense that O can sell it, give it away, or devise it. Further, if O dies without a will, the reversionary interest will pass to O's heirs. Thus, in both examples O's interest is presently alienable, inheritable, and devisable. O's interest is future in the sense that O is entitled to possession at a future point in time: the expiration of the prior estate.

If A in Example 2 dies survived by a son, S, S will inherit the fee tail. O will continue to own the reversion. If O dies leaving a will in favor of a child, C, C will hold the reversion. The relationship between C and S will be governed, in the absence of any contrary agreement between the two of them, by the law of waste.

Admittedly, it is far easier to appreciate the presence of a reversion when only a life estate is created in the grantee. The reversion present when only a fee tail is created, however, was apparently just as real to the early common law lawyers. For them, the dying out of a direct line was a common-enough occurrence to make the reversion after a fee tail an important future interest.

If O says nothing extra in creating the other two present estates, two similar but differently named future interests arise in O.

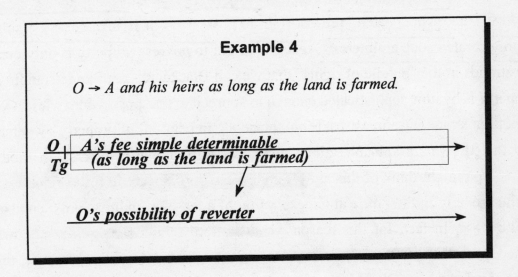

Example 4

O → A and his heirs as long as the land is farmed.

O
Tg *A's fee simple determinable (as long as the land is farmed)*

O's possibility of reverter

Don't be tempted to say "possibility of reversion." It will be important for you to distinguish reversions from possibilities of reverter.

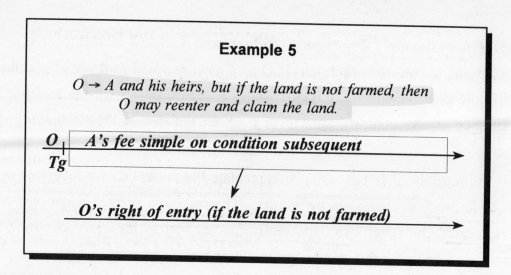

Example 5

O → A and his heirs, but if the land is not farmed, then O may reenter and claim the land.

A's fee simple on condition subsequent

O's right of entry (if the land is not farmed)

O's right of entry, recall, is also called a "power of termination." It will take effect only if the land is not farmed.

The possibility of reverter and the right of entry are classified as "future interests" because O has no present right to possession of Blackacre as a result of having created such an interest. Again, the right to *possess* property is only one of the strands in the "bundle of rights" that we call Blackacre. Your understanding of property is by now sophisticated enough to appreciate that possession, while a very important strand in some cases, is not the be-all and end-all of property ownership, and that O owns a valuable, albeit nonpossessory, property interest. In modern terms, you might think of this as similar to a landlord's right to re-take possession of the property in the future at the expiration of a lease or on breach of a condition in the lease. In fact, for this reason, your landlord's interest is sometimes today called a "reversionary" interest, or even a right of entry. Initially, however, there were restrictions on O's ability to transfer the possibility of reverter and the right of entry. The chart below summarizes the rules.

Summary of Transferability (Future Interests in the Grantor)

There are three future interests in the grantor, created automatically on creation of four of the five present, possessory estates: life estate, fee tail, fee simple determinable, and fee simple on condition subsequent. The following chart compares and contrasts the three future interests in the grantor.

	Reversion	*Possibility of Reverter*	*Right of Entry*
How created?	When O conveys an expirable estate, i.e., a fee tail or a life estate.	When O conveys a fee simple determinable.	When O conveys a fee simple on condition subsequent.
Alienable?	Yes	Not by gift or sale. With respect to a will, there is no clear authority.	No
Inheritable?	Yes	Yes	Yes

Most of these restrictions on alienation have been removed currently, by statute, but for the purposes of this discussion, we will consider both the possibility of reverter and the right of entry to be inalienable. The question of the devisability of a possibility of reverter depends on an interpretation of the Statute of Wills (1540), as amended in 1542, which provided for the devise of estates "in possession, reversion or remainder." Judicial opinion indicated that the statute did not include rights of entry. There is a scholarly dispute about the effect of the statute on possibilities of reverter. Some modern statutes appear to be attempts to clarify the common law rules; others are more straightforward. It is not clear whether the law of waste protected O's future interest in the case of a possibility of reverter or a right of entry.

Those are the future interests in the grantor; we'll be adding a detail here and there as we go, but that's most of what you need to know for now about reversions, reverters and rights of entry. Obviously, these interests have other legal aspects. For example, these interests create title problems for land owners when the language employed in a deed is unclear. Such interests may have estate tax consequences. Advanced property courses and advanced tax courses will involve practical problems in which the technical vocabulary you are acquiring should prove helpful. For our purposes, all you need to learn now are the concepts, the primary language by which such interests are created, and their significance within the general scheme of estates in land.

B.   Future Interests in a Grantee

You have seen that O may convey Blackacre to A and retain one of the future interests discussed above. The common law also allowed O, if O was careful to follow the rules, to convey a future interest to some third party, whom we shall, for the moment, call "B." Those common law rules, which developed early, were strict. If the rules were broken during the early common law period, the conveyance of the future interest was ineffective, and O ended up retaining, rather than conveying, a future interest.

We make two points before we lay out these rules. First, the bad news: These rules, though older than old—remember that we are still talking about times *before* 1536—are still important today. Crucial distinctions may still depend on the proper classification, and, while the case law and statutory principles governing construction of language in documents are much more flexible than they used to be, the rules that follow still influence the case law and thus are of significance in classification.

Second, and the good news, sort of: These rules are rules of law, not rules of construction and they do not require you to figure out the grantor's intent. These rules, if not followed, may in fact frustrate the grantor's intent.

The rules relative to creating future interests in a grantee before 1536 were:

Rule 1.   *Only expirable estates could be followed by a future interest in a grantee.*

Hence, only a fee tail or a life estate may be followed by such an interest. That's not hard to remember, since it is in those two cases that O has a reversion if the deed or will contains nothing extra. After creating a determinable fee or a fee simple on condition subsequent, on the other hand, O retains a future interest that O may not alienate and may not create in a third party. In other words, the common law permitted, reasonably enough, the "replacement" of an alienable reversion by a future interest in a third party. The future interest that follows these rules is called a "remainder." The person in whom the interest is created traditionally has been called a "remainderman." The fifth case, the fee simple absolute, is never followed by any future interest.

Rule 2.   *The future interest created in B must be capable of taking effect immediately upon expiration of the preceding estate.*

The simplest example of this is:

Example 6

O → A for life, then to B and his heirs.

A has a life estate; B has a remainder.

No symbol is given for this grant, because the symbol depends on the classification of the remainder, which we have not yet discussed.

Here are two future interests in B that do not satisfy this requirement:

Examples 7 and 8

O → A for life, and one year later to B and his heirs.

O → A for life, then to B ten years after A's death if B is still solvent.

In both cases the future interest will not be ready to take effect at expiration, A's death. Hence, the future interest in B is invalid before 1536. The state of the title, then, is this: A has a life estate and O has a reversion. B has nothing.

Here are two that will work:

Examples 9 and 10

O → A for life, then if B survives A, to B and his heirs.

O → A for life, then if B has married C, to B and his heirs.

In both cases, you see, B's future interest is ready to take effect (that is, the condition is ready to be tested) on A's death. B has a remainder in both cases. How about:

Example 11

O → A for life, then if B marries C either before or after A's death, to B and his heirs.

This future interest is not valid under the common law rules before 1536, since the condition is not verifiable at the expiration of A's life estate. A has a life estate; B has nothing; O has a reversion. Well, how about:

Example 12

O → A for life, then if B marries C, to B and his heirs.

Depending on how the condition is read, this conveyance looks like either Example 11 (hence invalid) or Example 10 (hence valid). What is done with a grant that might be read to be either valid or invalid? The common law judges held that a condition that *could* be read to be verifiable at A's death *should* be read that way. ***Purefoy v. Rogers***, 2 Wm. Saund. 380, 85 Eng. Rep. 1181 (1690). Thus, Example 12 creates a valid remainder in B because the condition is capable of being tested at A's death. If B has not married C by that time, B will not take possession of Blackacre; B's future interest will never become a present, possessory interest unless B marries C before A dies. This result involves the doctrine of destructibility of contingent remainders, discussed in detail later.

The third pre-1536 requirement for a future interest in a grantee is similar to the second:

Rule 3.   *The future interest created in B must not take effect before the expiration of the preceding estate.*

Example 12 (again)

O → A for life, then if B marries C, to B and his heirs.

B has a remainder.

Compare:

Example 13

O → A for life, then if B marries C while A is living, immediately to B and his heirs.

Here the condition as construed by the early common law cases would take effect before A's death, cutting short A's life estate, an impermissible grant before 1536. Since the grant cannot take effect as written, at early common law A had a life estate, B had nothing, and O had a reversion.

It is worth emphasizing that the phrase "but if" seemed to signal an impermissible "cutoff," whereas the word "if" received a radically different construction. "If" precedes a condition that may take effect at the expiration of the prior estate. Consider:

Example 14

O → A for life, but if B ever becomes President, then to B and his heirs.

Since the condition might be met either before, at, or after A's death, you might argue that the ***Purefoy*** case referred to above requires that we test the condition on expiration and preserve B's remainder. You would lose that argument to the heavy hand of grammar. "But if," said the common law, indicates an intention to cut short the life estate if B became President before A died, even though as the facts develop B may not become President until after A's death. B does not have a remainder. O has a reversion. [Incidentally, thanks for ignoring the anachronism. For the sake of variety, we will occasionally slip in grants involving people or institutions that didn't exist in the days we refer to.]

Here are some additional examples:

15. *O → A for life, then to B and his heirs.*

     B has a remainder.

16. *O → A and the heirs of his body, remainder to B and his heirs.*

     B has a remainder. Using the word "remainder" makes the future interest neither more nor less than a remainder.

17. *O → A and his heirs as long as A farms the land, then to B and his heirs.*

     B's interest follows a fee simple determinable, which does not expire. Thus B's interest is not a remainder and is void before 1536. B has nothing, A has a fee simple determinable, and O has a possibility of reverter.

18. *O → A for life and one year after A's death to B and his heirs.*

The one year wait is improper before 1536. The "remainder" is void, B has nothing, and O has a reversion.

19. *O → A for life, remainder one year after A's death to B and his heirs.*

The word "remainder" is improperly used and does not save the grant. As above, the wait makes the interest following the life estate void.

20. *O → A for life, then if B has married W, to B and his heirs.*

B's interest is ready to take effect, *i.e.*, the condition is ready to be tested, at A's death. B has a remainder.

21. *O → A for life, but if B marries W, then to B and his heirs.*

Here, B's interest does not take effect at expiration; therefore, no remainder. Notice the importance of the precise wording when this example is compared with the one immediately above. In other words, the sole difference between these two examples lies in the common law sense of "cutoff" suggested by Example 21.

22. *O → A for life, but if A should become Protestant, then to B and his heirs.*

The attempt to cut short A's life estate is improper before 1536. The "remainder" is void, B has nothing and O has a reversion.

23. *O → A for life, then to whoever is president of GM and his or her heirs.*

That future president of GM has a remainder even though the person to whom the remainder will belong is not identifiable at the time of the grant. If GM no longer exists at the death of A, the property will revert to O.

24. *O → A for life, then if B has reached the age of 21, to B and his heirs.*

B's interest follows an expirable estate, doesn't cut it short, and the grant with **the condition** is ready to be applied at the expiration of A's life estate. Therefore, B has a remainder.

25. *O → A for life, remainder to A's heir and his heirs.*

A's heir, unidentifiable if A is alive, has a remainder.

*Compare Example 25 with "O → A and his heirs." Can you see the difference between the two conveyances? What may A sell in the quoted example? In example 25? These two conveyances, which you have just found to be not equivalent, are made equivalent by the venerable Rule in **Shelley's Case**, discussed in Chapter Six.*

After deciding whether a conveyance creates a remainder, two tasks must be done to complete the analysis of the future interest. First you must decide what *present* estate the remainder will become if it ever becomes *possessory*. That is, if B has a future interest in Blackacre, which of the five present, possessory estates will B have if and when he is able to possess Blackacre? For example:

26.   *O → A for life, then to B for life.*

      B has a remainder in a life estate.

27.   *O → A for life, then to B and his heirs.*

      B has a remainder in fee simple.

28.   *O → A for life, then to B and his heirs as long as he remains unmarried.*

      B has a remainder in fee simple determinable.

That is easy enough; one just looks for the same clues in classifying the remainder as in classifying a present, possessory estate.

The second task is to classify the remainder by type. There were two primary categories of remainders at common law: vested remainders and contingent remainders. We discuss vested remainders first.

1. Vested Remainders

X is said to have a vested remainder if X has a remainder and:

(a)   X is a person born and ascertainable, and

(b)   There is no condition other than expiration of the preceding estate that must be met before X's interest may come into possession.

Example 29

O → A for life, then to B and his heirs.

O | *A's life estate* | *B's vested remainder in fee simple* →
Tg | | Ex

You should satisfy yourself that the symbol above is accurate: (1) that B's future interest is, indeed, a remainder; (2) that B's remainder is in fee simple; and (3) that B's remainder is vested.

Here are some examples of vested and non-vested remainders:

30.   *O → A for life, then to A's youngest child living at the time of A's death and that child's heirs.*

It is impossible to determine, until A dies, who will be his youngest child then living. Therefore, although there may be a very likely candidate (suppose A is 92 at the time of grant), the actual taker cannot yet be ascertained; hence the remainder is not vested.

31.   *O → A for life, then to B and his heirs.* (B is an identifiable, living person at *Tg*.)

No problem; B has a vested remainder in fee simple.

> *In this book—and probably in your class—when a letter is used to indicate a person, we'll assume the designated person is born and ascertainable. When we want to indicate otherwise, we'll describe the person's characteristics, as in Examples 30 and 32.*

32.   *O → A for life, then to the very first child born in New York City on the day of A's death and that child's heirs.*

The child is unborn and therefore its remainder is not vested.

33.   *O → A and the heirs of his body, then to B's heir and his heirs. (B is living.)*

A living person has no heir, only *potential* heirs, so B's heir is unascertained. Thus, B's heir's remainder is not vested. It does not violate Rule 2 above because B may die before the prior estate ends; in that case, B's heir would be capable of being determined in time.

34.   *O → A for life, then to B and his heirs as long as the land is farmed.*

The condition is understood to be on B's possession, not on his taking. There is no condition that must be satisfied in order for B to come into possession. Therefore, B's remainder is vested; it is a vested remainder in fee simple determinable.

35.   *O → A for life, then if B has agreed to farm the land, to B and his heirs.*

Compare with the example immediately above. Here the condition must be satisfied before B may come into possession, thus the remainder is not vested.

Vested remainders were considered quite substantial interests at common law. A vested remainder was alienable inter vivos, it was inheritable, and it was devisable.

2. Contingent Remainders

Remainders that are not vested are called contingent. Thus, X is said to have a contingent remainder if X has a remainder and:

(a)   X is unborn or unascertainable, or

(b)   There is a condition that must be satisfied before X may come into possession. Such a condition is called a "condition precedent." Since X has a remainder, we know that the condition precedent must be able to be tested at the expiration of the preceding estate.

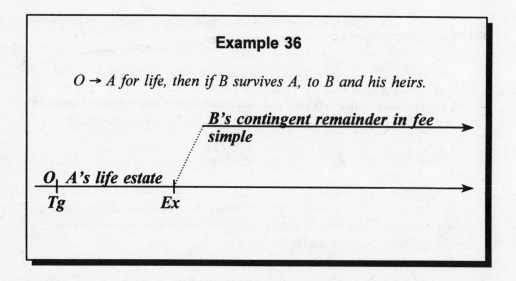

Example 36

O → A for life, then if B survives A, to B and his heirs.

B's contingent remainder in fee simple

O *A's life estate*
Tg   *Ex*

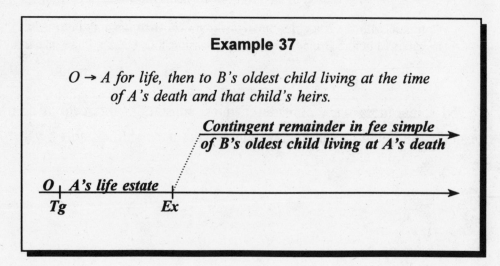

Example 37

O → A for life, then to B's oldest child living at the time of A's death and that child's heirs.

Contingent remainder in fee simple of B's oldest child living at A's death

O *A's life estate*
Tg   *Ex*

We experienced some difficulty in attributing ownership of the contingent remainder in Example 37, because the remainderman is unascertainable, which is exactly the reason the remainder is contingent. Suppose B's oldest child at *Tg* is S. Does S have a contingent remainder? No, S has merely an expectation—a *hope*, really—of meeting the condition imposed by O. When a remainderman is unascertainable, those who might become the remainderman have *expectancies*, not contingent remainders. Because the remainder "belongs" to a fictitious, as-yet unascertainable person, perhaps you will find it easier to characterize the owner by using the description contained in the document. In Example 37, then, O has created a contingent remainder in favor of "B's oldest child living at A's death."

You noticed, we hope, the unassigned chunk of Blackacre in both the diagrams in Examples 36 and 37. This is a new future interest—that which follows a contingent remainder—and it is just another form of reversion. In other words, if the condition is not met, or if the remainderman/woman is not born or ascertainable when A dies and A's life estate expires, then O regains the land. Thus, the complete symbol:

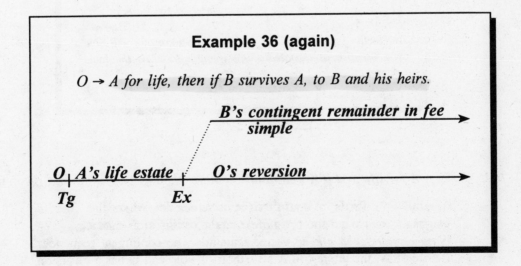

Example 36 (again)

O → A for life, then if B survives A, to B and his heirs.

B's contingent remainder in fee simple

O A's life estate   O's reversion
Tg   *Ex*

Here are some other examples of contingent remainders:

38.   *O → A and the heirs of his body, then if B is still living, to B and his heirs.*

B has a contingent remainder in fee simple.

39.   *O → A for life, then if B has married C, to B and his heirs.*

B has a contingent remainder in fee simple.

40.   *O → A for life, then to A's firstborn child and that child's heirs.*

If A has children, the remainderman is known and the remainder is vested. If A has no children, then O has created a contingent remainder in fee simple in favor of A's unborn "first born."

> *In order to classify this grant you had to know some facts— whether A has any children—that were not contained in the grant itself. This is often the case in real life as well as in this book and in class. In this book, we—or your teacher in class—will give you the information that you need. Note, too, that because the classification depends on facts outside the grant, and because those facts are inherently subject to change, the classification of the estates in a grant is subject to change over time. Here, for example, the remainder will change from contingent to vested—it will "vest," we say—on the birth of A's first child. As the pages go on, we will give you practice at repeatedly classifying estates as the facts change.*

41.   *O → A for life, but if A's firstborn is male, then to that child and his heirs.*

Careful! A's firstborn doesn't have a remainder, since the "but if" language seeks to cut short A's life estate in certain circumstances. There is **no remainder at all**: no vested remainder, no contingent remainder. Before 1536, the interest in A's firstborn is void and O has a reversion.

There is a special type of contingent remainder called the alternative contingent remainder. X and Y are said to have alternative contingent remainders if:

(a) X has a contingent remainder, and

(b) X's remainder is followed immediately by Y's future interest, which is a remainder and which takes effect in exactly those circumstances in which X's remainder will not.

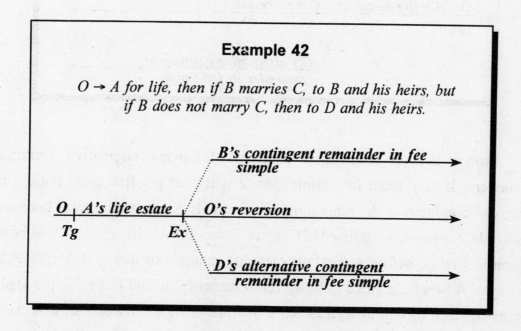

Example 42

*O → A for life, then if B marries C, to B and his heirs, but
if B does not marry C, then to D and his heirs.*

Here are those words "but if" that you may have begun to think of as the clue that you are dealing with a non-remainder. That is good thinking, but this is an exception to that otherwise sound rule. "But if" means non-remainder (and void before 1536) **unless** it introduces a condition precedent that is the opposite of the earlier condition precedent. Then you have alternative contingent remainders.

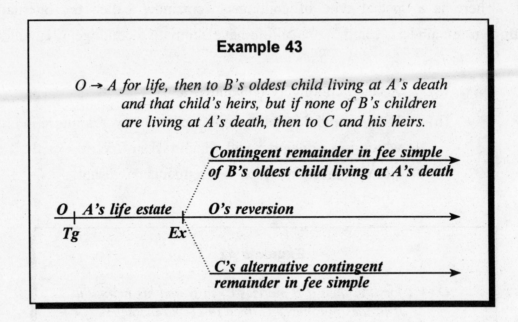

Example 43

O → A for life, then to B's oldest child living at A's death and that child's heirs, but if none of B's children are living at A's death, then to C and his heirs.

Contingent remainder in fee simple of B's oldest child living at A's death

O A's life estate O's reversion

Tg Ex

C's alternative contingent remainder in fee simple

Notice that O still has a reversion following alternative contingent remainders. It may seem impossible that O will ever get Blackacre back, since either one condition or the other must be met. This is not strictly true, because it is possible, for reasons discussed in Chapter Three, for A's life estate to end before it expires (that is, before A dies). The easiest example of this is if A refuses the life estate. A beneficiary of a gift may refuse to accept it, and that principle applies to gifts by deed or will as well as those that are made by delivery of possession. In such circumstances, because the conditions on the alternative contingent remainders are to be tested only at expiration and, thus, neither is ready to take effect, O's reversion becomes possessory and O has a fee simple.

Contingent remainders were not considered very substantial interests at common law. A contingent remainder was not alienable inter vivos. It was, however, inheritable and it might be devised.

Some reminders on remainders:

1. Whether a remainder is contingent or vested often depends upon information not included in the grant. For example, consider:

Example 44

O → A for life, then if B has married C, to B and his heirs.

The classification of B's remainder depends upon B's marital status. If B has married C, then we know that when A dies, the condition will be met. Hence, if A is alive and B has married C, B's remainder is vested. On the other hand, if B and C are not married, then B's remainder is contingent.

Obviously, then, it is possible for a remainder to change from contingent to vested (but not from vested to contingent), and it might do so depending on facts not included in the grant. Later on, we will give you some problems involving such changing conditions. In the meantime, we will give you all the relevant facts as of the time of the grant and ask for analysis only under that set of facts.

2. Remember, before classifying the remainder, make sure the future interest *is* a remainder.

3. Make sure you have accounted for all future interests in any grant. There may be more than one:

Example 45

O → A for life, then to B for life, then to C for life.

O	A's life estate	B's vested remainder for life	C's vested remainder for life	O's reversion
Tg		Ex	Ex	Ex

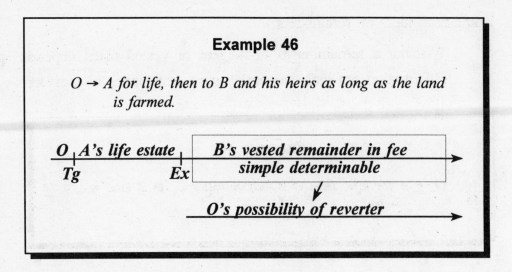

Example 46

$O \rightarrow A$ for life, then to B and his heirs as long as the land is farmed.

O | A's life estate | B's vested remainder in fee simple determinable
Tg   **Ex**

O's possibility of reverter

What has been described thus far is a system that emerged over several hundred years, at least. The rules governing the definition of a remainder and distinguishing vested and contingent remainders actually represent the three conveyancing rules that property lawyers observed at common law. Apparently these rules were not unlike modern tax statutes that prohibit or discourage certain tax-avoidance devices property planners otherwise would attempt.

It is not necessary to explore the feudal economic and social structure the preservation of which led to the common law rules of conveyancing. It is enough to suggest that the common law rules of conveyancing produced the limits on that future interest in a grantee known as a remainder. These limits are perhaps best understood as the definition of a remainder, only explicable historically.

What you have been exposed to in Chapters One and Two is a system of five present interests and five future interests permitted by the common law courts before the early sixteenth century. We summarize in the following chart. After you have looked over this chart, try your new intellectual equipment on the problem set. The answers immediately follow the set. You will meet in subsequent chapters one more present, possessory interest and one more future interest, for a final total of a dozen.

C.   Review Materials

1.   Summary of present and future interests before 1536

PRESENT POSSESSORY ESTATE	FUTURE ESTATE	
	Grantor	Grantee
Fee Simple Absolute	NONE	NONE
Fee Tail	Reversion	Remainder
Life Estate	Reversion	Remainder
Fee Simple Determinable	Possibility of Reverter	NONE
Fee Simple on Condition Subsequent	Right of Entry (Power of Termination)	NONE

2.   Summary of transferability

[*Strictly speaking, land could generally not be devised until after the Statute of Wills was enacted in 1540. The "Devisable" column below gives the rules for the post-1540 devise of the pre-1536 interests.*]

Present Interests	Alienable	Devisable	Inheritable
Fee Simple Absolute	Yes	Yes	Yes
Fee Tail	Limited	No	Modified
Life Estate (other than life estate *pur autre vie*)	Yes	No	No
Fee Simple Determinable	Yes	Yes	Yes
Fee Simple on Condition Subsequent	Yes	Yes	Yes

Future Interests	*Alienable*	*Devisable*	*Inheritable*
Reversion	Yes	Yes	Yes
Possibility of Reverter	No	Probably not*	Yes
Right of Entry	No	No	Yes
Remainder— 　Vested 　Contingent	 Yes No	 Yes Yes	 Yes Yes

*The answer here depends on an interpretation of the original English Statute of Wills (1540), as amended in 1542. The Statute provided for the devise of estates "in possession, reversion or remainder." There is some authority that possibilities of reverter, like rights of entry, were not within the 1542 amendment. Other authorities are not satisfied this is so. **See** L. Simes & A. Smith, **The Law of Future Interests** § 1901, at 200 (2d ed. 1956).

D. Review Problem Set

1. Give the "state of the title" in each of the grants below, that is to say, tell what present or future interest in the land each of the parties has at *Tg*.

> **HINT:** *Although we have listed O first, you may find it easier to name the other interests first, before deciding what, if anything, O has retained.*

a. $O \rightarrow A$.

O has ~~reversion Fee Simple At~~.

A has ~~life estate~~.

b. $O \rightarrow A$ *in fee simple absolute.*

O has ~~reversion; fee simple ab.~~.

A has ~~life estate~~.

c. $O \rightarrow A$ *and the male heirs of his body.*

O has ~~reversion~~.

A has ~~fee tail male~~.

    d.   *O → A for life, then to B and his heirs.* [B is O's older brother, alive at *Tg*.]

        O has ___*re nothing*___.

        A has ___*life estate*___.

        B has ___*vested remainder in fee simple*___

    e.   *O → A for life, then if A dies unmarried, to B and his heirs, otherwise to W for life.*

        O has ___*reversion*___.

        A has ___*life estate*___.

        B has ___*contingent remainder in fee simple*___

        W has ___*alternative contingent*___ *remainder in life estate*

2.   In each case below, what is B's interest? The time of the grant is 1530.

    a.   *O → B and his heirs.* *fee simple absolute*

    b.   *O → B and his heirs as long as the fences stay in good repair.* *fee simple determinable*

c. *O → B and his heirs, but if a Democrat is ever elected President, O may reenter and reclaim the land.* fee simple on condition subsequent

But if - electors?

d. *O → B and the heirs of his body.* Fee tail,

e. *O → A and his heirs. [B is A's oldest boy, alive and well at Tg.]* B has nothing - expectancy.

f. *O → A for life, then if B marries C, to C and her heirs.* B has nothing - curtsey as husband

g. *O → A for life, then if B marries C, to B and his heirs.*
Fee Simple on Condition Subsequent;
If B married to C then vested remainder
If B not married to C - contingent remainder in fee simple

h. *O → A and his heirs, but if the land is ever used for commercial purposes, to B and his heirs.*
B has nothing But if + remainder = NO remainder reversion to O

i. *O → A for life, then to W for life, then, if Z is still alive, to C for life, otherwise to B and his heirs.*
alternative contingent remainder in fee simple

3. In each case below, O is your client. If possible, construct a grant that will dispose of her property in the way she desires. If it can't be done, explain why.

a. O wants her friend A to have a fee simple absolute.
O to A and her heirs.

b. O wants A to have a fee simple—"almost"; i.e., she never wants the land to be used for commercial purposes.
O to A and her heirs, As long as the land is never used for commercial purposes.

c. O wants A to have a fee simple, unless and until B returns from Rome, in which case she wants B to have a fee simple.

Grant – But if –

d. O wants her son to have the land until he dies and afterwards she wants it to return to her, unless she is dead, in which case she wants it to go to her heirs.

O to A ss.
O to A for life

e. O would like to let A have the land while A is alive. After A dies, O wants the land to go either to B or to C depending on who gets married first—O wants the land to go to the first of the two to marry.

O to A for life, then to the first of B & C to marry or –C.
their heirs

f. O wants her friend A to have the land for A's lifetime and then she wants it to go to her friend B's youngest son, but only if B marries C. If B doesn't marry C, then O wants the land to go to the Catholic Church, but only for as long as it is used for church purposes.

O to A for life, then to the youngest male heir of B, provided B
marries C, But if B is not married to C, to the Catholic Church, its
successors and assigns for as long as it is used for church purposes.

g. O wants the land to go to A and stay in A's direct family line.

O to A and the heirs of his body.

4. What does the following statute mean?

> Unless a different purpose appears by express words or by necessary inference, every estate in land created by deed or will, without words of inheritance, shall be deemed an estate in fee simple.

If in question, the assumption is a
fee simple absolute
makes "and his heirs" unnecessary

5.   Classify the first future interest in each of the conveyances below as either:

a.   None; the future interest is illegal, void or meaningless before 1536;

b.   A vested remainder; or

c.   A contingent remainder.

(1)   __b__   O → A for life, then to B and his heirs.
                   [B is alive and well.]

(2)   __a__   O → A and his heirs, then to B and his *nothing left to grant* heirs. [B is alive and well.]

(3)   __c__   O → A for life, then to B's oldest child living at A's death.

(4)   __A__   O → A and his heirs, but if the land is not farmed, to B and his heirs.

(5)   __c__   O → A for life, then if X has married Y, to C and his heirs, but if X has not married Y, then to B and his heirs.

Answers to Review Problem Set

1. Give the "state of the title" in each of the grants below (that is to say, tell what present or future interest in the land each of the parties has at *Tg*).

    a. $O \rightarrow A$.

    O has a reversion.
    A has a life estate.

    b. $O \rightarrow A$ *in fee simple absolute*.

    O has a reversion.
    A has a life estate. (Remember, the magic words "and his heirs" were
     required at common law.)

    c. $O \rightarrow A$ *and the male heirs of his body*.

    O has a reversion.
    A has a fee tail male.

    d. $O \rightarrow A$ *for life, then to B and his heirs*. [B is O's older
     brother, alive at *Tg*.]

    O has nothing.
    A has a life estate.
    B has a vested remainder in fee simple.

    e. $O \rightarrow A$ *for life, then if A dies unmarried, to B and his heirs,
     otherwise to W for life*.

    O has a reversion.
    A has a life estate.
    B has a contingent remainder in fee simple.
    W has an alternative contingent remainder in a life estate.

2.   In each case below, what is B's interest? The time of the grant is 1530.

a.   *O → B and his heirs.*

B has a fee simple.

b.   *O → B and his heirs as long as the fences stay in good repair.*

B has a fee simple determinable.

c.   *O → B and his heirs, but if a Democrat is ever elected President, O may reenter and reclaim the land.*

B has a fee simple on condition subsequent. (Once again, it was friendly of you to avoid comment on the anachronism.)

d.   *O → B and the heirs of his body.*

B has a fee tail.

e.   *O → A and his heirs.* [B is A's oldest boy, alive and well at **Tg**.]

B has nothing. B only has an expectancy, not considered a property interest, that he will be entitled to the property when A dies.

f.   *O → A for life, then if B marries C, to C and her heirs.*

B has nothing. This one might properly be called a "trick question." Note that there is no **grant** at all to B. We did not mean for you to wonder about any property rights that B gets by being C's husband.

g.   *O → A for life, then if B marries C, to B and his heirs.*

B's interest depends on B's marital status. Assuming that B is unmarried, B has a contingent remainder in fee simple. If B is married to C, then the remainder is vested. If B has married someone else, then the remainder is contingent, as B might still divorce that person and marry C.

h.   *O → A and his heirs, but if the land is ever used for commercial purposes, to B and his heirs.*

B has nothing. The "but if" language purports to cut short A's interest, so the interest O attempted to give B is void before 1536.

i.   *O → A for life, then to W for life, then, if Z is still alive, to C for life, otherwise to B and his heirs.*

B has an alternative contingent remainder in fee simple.

3.   In each case below, O is your client. If possible, construct a grant that will dispose of her property in the way she desires. If it can't be done, explain why.

a.   O wants her friend A to have a fee simple absolute.

O → A and her heirs.

b.   O wants A to have a fee simple—"almost"; i.e., she never wants the land to be used for commercial purposes.

O → A and his heirs as long as the land is not used for commercial purposes.

c.   O wants A to have a fee simple, unless and until B returns from Rome, in which case she wants B to have a fee simple.

This is not possible at common law before 1536.

d.   O wants her son to have the land until he dies and afterwards she wants it to return to her, unless she is dead, in which case she wants it to go to her heirs.

O → Son for life.

e.   O would like to let A have the land while A is alive. After A dies, O wants the land to go either to B or to C depending on who gets married first—O wants the land to go to the first of the two to marry.

O → A for life, and then to the first of B and C to marry and that person's heirs.

We guess that you might have tried this, which would have done just as well:

> *O → A for life, then to B and his heirs, if B marries before C does, but if C marries first, then to C and his heirs.*

Note that in both cases, O has a reversion, which will become possessory if neither B nor C has married at the time of A's death.

---

f.   O wants her friend A to have the land for A's lifetime and then she wants it to go to her friend B's youngest son, but only if B marries C. If B doesn't marry C, then O wants the land to go to the Catholic Church, but only for as long as it is used for church purposes.

> *O → A for life, then if B marries C, to B's youngest son, but if B doesn't marry C, to the Church as long as the land is used for church purposes.*

g.   O wants the land to go to A and stay in A's direct family line.

> *O → A and the heirs of his body.*

4.   What does the following statute mean?

> Unless a different purpose appears by express words or by necessary inference, every estate in land created by deed or will, without words of inheritance, shall be deemed an estate in fee simple.

This statute makes the words "and his heirs" unnecessary for the creation of a fee simple. Such statutes are common now. *See, e.g.,* CAL. CIV. CODE § 1105 (West 1982).

5. Classify the first future interest in each of the conveyances below as either:

   a.   None; the future interest is illegal, void or meaningless before 1536;

   b.   A vested remainder; or

   c.   A contingent remainder.

   (1) __b__ *O → A for life, then to B and his heirs.*
         [B is alive and well.]

   (2) __a__ *O → A and his heirs, then to B and his heirs.*
         [B is alive and well.]

   (3) __c__ *O → A for life, then to B's oldest child living at A's death.*

   (4) __a__ *O → A and his heirs, but if the land is not farmed, to B and his heirs.*

   (5) __c__ *O → A for life, then if X has married Y, to C and his heirs, but if X has not married Y, then to B and his heirs.*

CHAPTER THREE

THE FAMILY OF REMAINDERS

To this point you have learned several new concepts, including the general concept of a remainder, which is the subject of further exploration in this chapter. The word "remainder" refers to a future interest created in a grantee after an expirable estate in compliance with certain rules.

You also learned in the previous chapter that remainders are of two basic types: vested and contingent. For reasons similar to those that restricted the evolution of the concept of a remainder, the evolution of the two types of remainders was slow. The contingent remainder was recognized much later than its sibling, the vested remainder. Further, as indicated earlier, the contingent remainder was considered inalienable inter vivos; perhaps the factors that influenced its late recognition influenced the concept that it was inalienable. Finally, the contingent remainder had a very special attribute, or property: it was a destructible interest. The doctrine of destructibility of contingent remainders reflects the special, congenital disability shared by all contingent remainders at common law, which was not present in vested remainders.

A. The Doctrine of Destructibility of Contingent Remainders

The general property of destructibility shared by all contingent remainders is stated as follows:

> A contingent remainder is destroyed unless it vests at or before the termination of the preceding estate. If a remainder is destroyed, then, at the expiration of the preceding estate, the next vested estate comes into possession. This is usually the reversion.

This is easier to illustrate by example, however, than by statement. Suppose, for example:

Example 1

O → A for life, then to B and his heirs if B marries C.

Using the graphical symbolism, we might sketch:

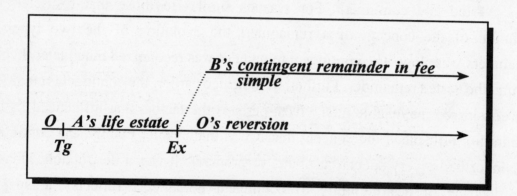

Now, suppose that B dies unmarried. In this example, it is relatively easy to see that the contingent aspect of B's gift prevents B or anyone claiming through B from having any claim to Blackacre; B is no longer able to satisfy the condition. The state of the title after B's death is: A has a life estate and O has a reversion. B's interest has been eliminated or destroyed by failing to satisfy the contingency upon which it was dependent. Symbolically:

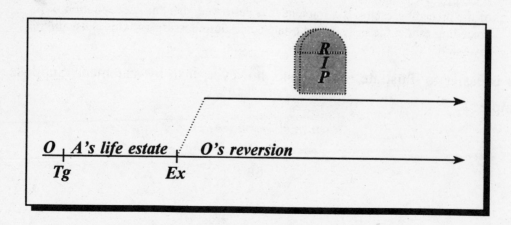

Or, more simply:

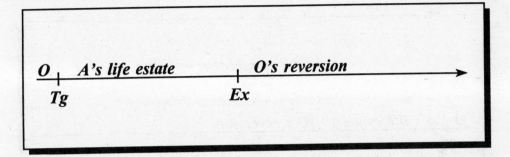

Notice that although, generally, contingent remainders are said to be devisable and inheritable, some conditions will impose an express or implied condition of survivorship. When this happens, the contingent remainder is neither devisable nor inheritable because it is contingent on not dying, an event indispensable to a valid disposition by will or succession by one's heirs. Conditions of survivorship are not the primary focus of this chapter. However, an example may be useful. If **"O → A for life, then to B and his heirs if B reaches 21,"** then B has an interest that is subject to an implied condition of survivorship. If B dies at age 10, his contingent remainder disappears. The condition B must meet has become impossible for B—or anyone else—to perform.

Probably for reasons associated with the same rules that generally restricted the meaning of a remainder, the common law courts found destruction had occurred in other instances not quite so easy to see. These additional instances are all part of the attribute of a contingent remainder we call destructibility.

Suppose, for example, that O conveyed as above:

Example 1 (again)

O → A for life, then to B and his heirs if B marries C.

Again, the symbolic representation is:

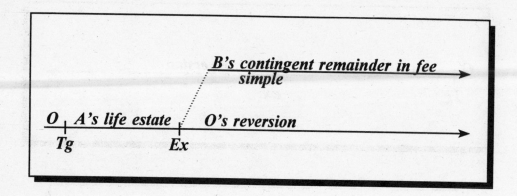

Suppose now, however, that A dies and B is still living and unmarried. B's interest disappeared at common law because it was said to be destroyed by its "failure to vest" before the expiration of the prior estate. A contingent remainder required the continuation of a preceding expirable estate, such as a life estate or a fee tail; if the preceding estate ended, the contingent remainderman/woman had to have satisfied the condition that made the estate contingent, or the interest was destroyed.

As suggested by the prior example, if B's interest disappeared, O's reversion replaced it. Likewise in this example, if B has not married C by the time A dies, O's reversion will become possessory and O will have a fee simple absolute. B will never take, even if he subsequently marries C. Symbolically:

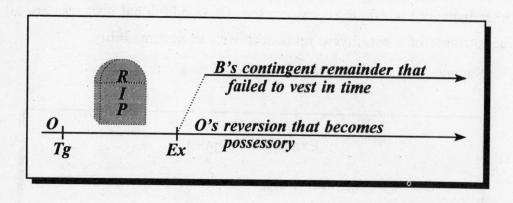

Or:

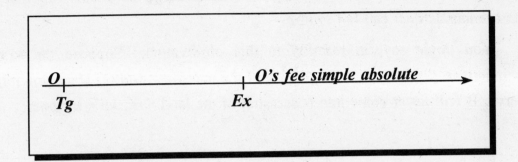

Using the same example for yet a third set of facts, suppose that B marries C while A is living. Now the graph changes dramatically:

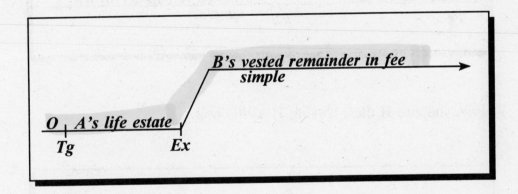

Or, more simply:

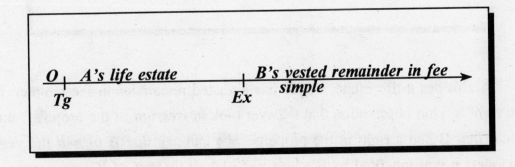

Vested remainders are indestructible. Because the taker is born and identifiable, and there is no condition precedent to taking, there is no way that the vested remainderman can fail to take.

You might say, in reaction to this observation, "Suppose the vested remainderman dies before the expiration of the preceding estate." If so, you might observe, B will never come into possession of the land. OK, let's try one:

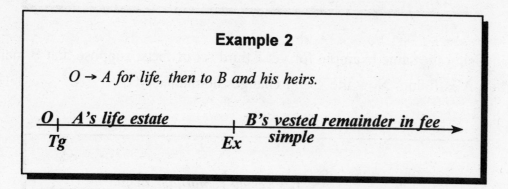

Now, suppose B dies, leaving H as his heir.

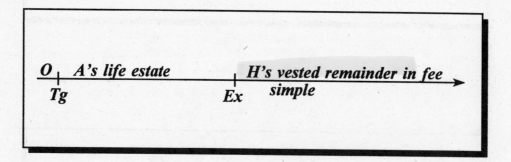

A still has a life estate, and H has a vested remainder in fee simple. You were right in your observation that B never took *possession* of the property, but it is clear that B had a right in the property. We can say that B *owned* the vested remainder; it was inherited by B's heir just like all the rest of B's property.

Earlier, we made the point without amplification that a vested remainder could never become contingent, although a transformation in the other direction was both possible and common. Do you see why? Take this conveyance:

Example 3

O → A for life, then, if B marries C, to B and his heirs.

If B is unmarried and A is alive, the diagram looks like this:

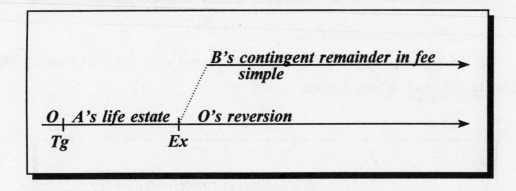

Now, suppose B marries C. The contingent remainder vests:

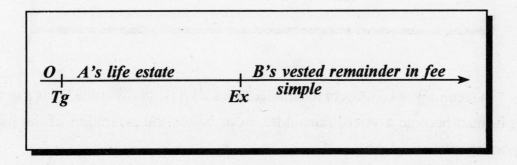

Now, you might want to say, suppose B divorces C, putting aside how difficult it was to get divorced back in the days we're talking about. Does the vested remainder "unvest" and become contingent? No. In O's original grant, he did not require that B *remain* married to C, or still be married to C at the time of A's death. So, B has met the condition and the remainder is vested for all time.

Now, suppose that O had put the more careful condition on B's remainder:

Example 4

O → A for life, then, if B marries and is still married to C on A's death, to B and his heirs.

On B's marriage to C, the remainder does *not* vest, for the condition now can't be tested until A dies. Hence,

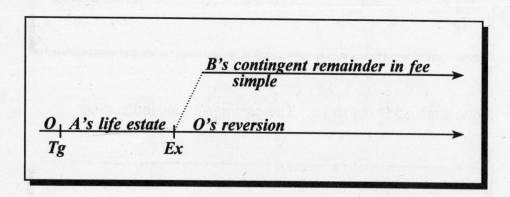

In summary, a contingent remainder, because it is "destructible," has a deadline; it must become a vested remainder on or before the expiration of the prior supporting estate.

> *A remainder may vest* **at** *expiration. For example, consider* **O → A for life, then if B survives A, to B and his heirs.** *Thus, it is technically incorrect to say that a remainder must vest* **before** *expiration.*

The estate that precedes and supports a contingent remainder will be a life estate or a fee tail. It can end in three ways: expiration, merger, or forfeiture.

1. Destruction of a Contingent Remainder at the Expiration of the Prior Estate

Suppose:

Example 5

O → A for life, then to the first son of A who reaches 21 and his heirs.

Suppose further that A dies leaving a son, 16. The contingent remainder is destroyed. O's reversion becomes possessory. The state of the title in this fact pattern, after A's death, is fee simple absolute in O.

As a review of the idea that a contingent remainder must vest in timely fashion, and as a review of other attributes of a contingent remainder, here is another example, a conveyance that produces a life estate followed by an alternative contingent remainder in fee:

Example 6

O → S for life, then to A and his heirs if A marries S and, if A fails to marry S, then to B and his heirs.

Assume for the first hypothetical that O, S, A, and B are all living.

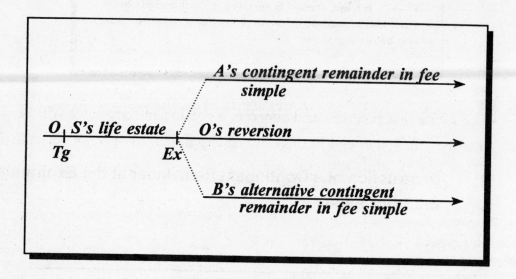

For the first modification of the hypothetical, assume that B dies, without a will, leaving D as his heir. The answer is illustrated by substituting "D" for "B," because B's contingent remainder is inheritable. (Note that the condition does not require B to do anything, so there is no implied condition of survivorship.)

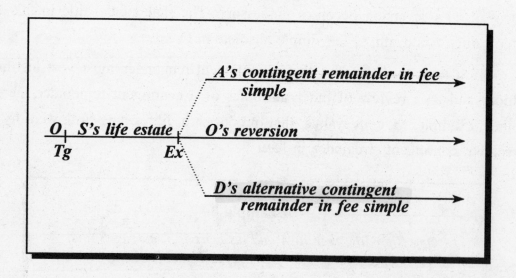

For the next modification of the hypothetical, assume that A marries S. The graph changes radically:

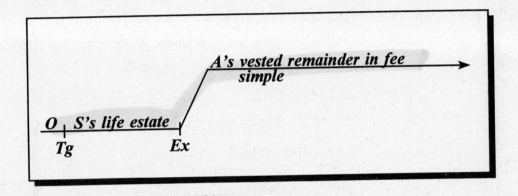

Finally, S dies, and the graph changes again:

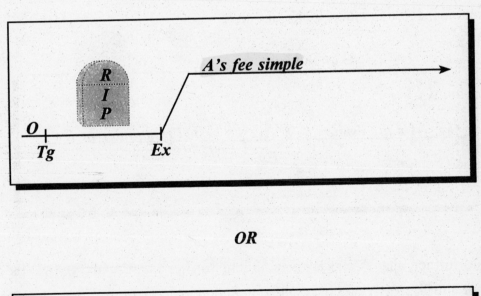

2. Destruction of a Contingent Remainder at the Termination of the Prior, Supporting Estate by Merger

The concept of merger in property law has broader application than its contribution to the law of contingent remainders. As a general principle, merger treats separate interests that belong to one person, under some circumstances, as having combined into a larger interest. For example, suppose:

Example 7

O → A for life, then to B and his heirs.

Our graphical representation looks like this:

```
O |  A's life estate          |  B's vested remainder in fee
Tg                            Ex   simple →
```

Suppose, further, that A and B each sells his or her interest to X. X holds a life estate for the life of A and a vested remainder in fee simple. The common law employed the concept known as merger to explain that X has a fee simple. The principle of merger was applied in order to reclassify the two lesser interests X purchased into the greater interest of a fee simple absolute.

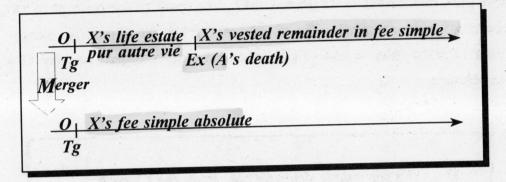

As another example, suppose:

Example 8

O → the Church, its successors and assigns* as long as the land is used as a church.

*"Successors and assigns" takes the place of "and his heirs" for institutions, which have no "heirs."

This conveyance is graphically represented as:

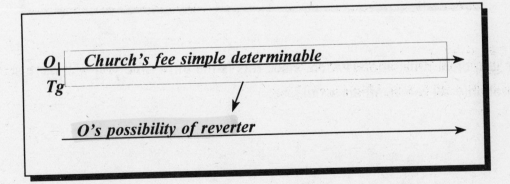

Suppose the Church releases its interest to O. As a result of the concept of merger, the common law recognized a fee simple in O after the Church's release. The Church's released interest and O's retained interest "merged" to give O a fee simple absolute.

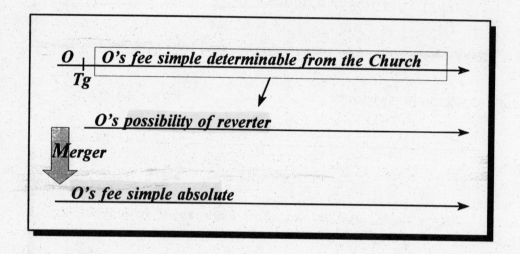

Now, suppose:

Example 1 (yet again)

O → A for life, then to B and his heirs if B marries C.

Our graphical illustration (which, since this is the third time you will have seen it, is probably all too familiar) would be:

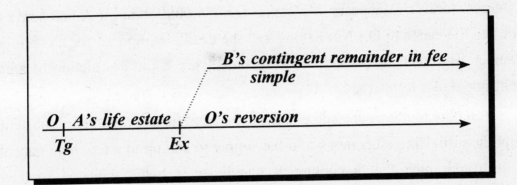

Suppose, while A is living and B is unmarried, never having married, O conveys the reversion to A.

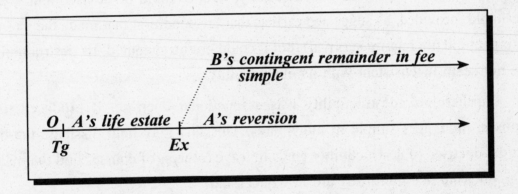

Here, too, the common law courts "saw" or "felt" or "decreed," if you prefer, that the life estate and reversion would combine into a fee simple. Once that happened, B's contingent remainder, not having a life estate to support it, would be destroyed. Poof! A has a fee simple absolute, and B has nothing.

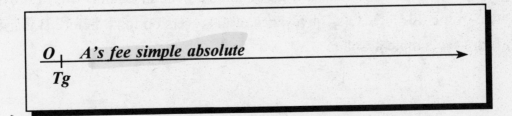

B's interest forever disappears. (A similar result would obtain if A had conveyed his or her life estate to O.) Not having met the deadline imposed for a contingent remainder, B's interest disappears for all time. This is the destruction of a contingent remainder by merger.

You may find it troublesome that a life estate and a reversion are substantial enough or sufficient components of a fee simple to add up to a fee. You may also find it troublesome that a contingent remainder is being defeated somewhat cavalierly and mystically. Both of these ideas seem fair criticism in the rational light of the twentieth century. However, apparently the contingent remainder as it eventually emerged in the catalogue of estates in land and future interests was closer to what we might call an expectancy; true, it could be devised and it was inheritable (provided, as suggested earlier, that the condition that made the interest contingent did not require survival), but it could not be alienated. Its destructibility does not seem inconsistent with its inalienability.

Furthermore, destructibility was a functional doctrine. It produced, one supposes, more fees simple in individuals. This fact may help dissipate the bad taste the doctrine of destructibility tends to leave (others, of course, find the magic of the doctrine one more treasure in wonderland).

By now, you might appreciate a definition of merger: The doctrine of merger provides that if successive vested estates come into the same hands, the two estates are transformed into the largest possible interest. Therefore, in the above examples, since the requisites for merger exist, A has a fee simple absolute. The life estate ended by merger at a time when the contingent remainder in B was not ready to take. Thus, at common law, the contingent remainder in B was destroyed. The state of the title after O's conveyance of his reversion to A, before B married C: A has a fee simple absolute.

Symbolically:

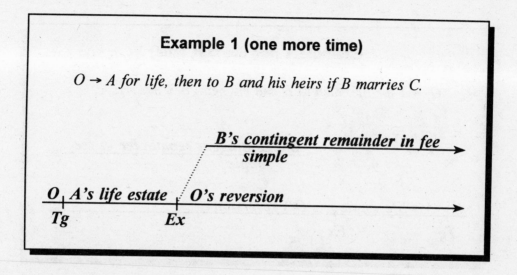

O conveys his reversion to A:

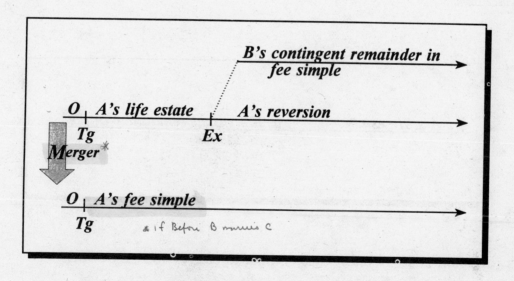

On the other hand, assume B marries C before A dies. B's remainder vests and may not be destroyed by any action of A or O. The state of the title is now life estate in A, vested remainder in B. O's reversion is destroyed.

Symbolically:

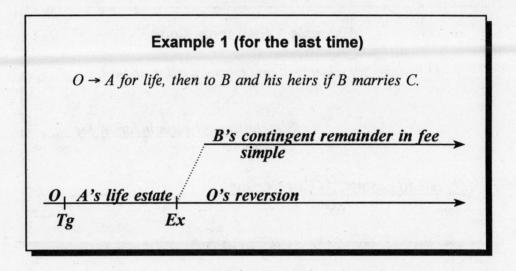

B marries C:

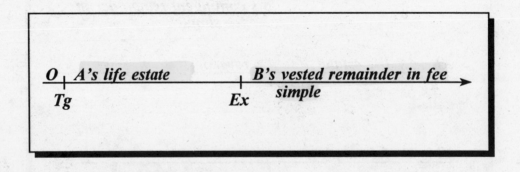

O's reversion is destroyed; O has nothing to convey to A.

3. Destruction of a Contingent Remainder by the Termination of the Prior Estate by Forfeiture

Suppose:

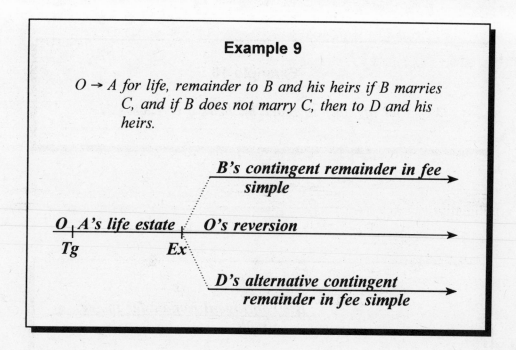

Example 9

O → A for life, remainder to B and his heirs if B marries C, and if B does not marry C, then to D and his heirs.

At common law some offenses, called felonies, carried a penalty of forfeiture of property. Assume A commits a felony and thereby forfeits the life estate before B marries C. In that case, A's life estate has ended prematurely and the contingent remainders are destroyed. The state of the title after A's forfeiture: O has a fee simple absolute.

If one assumes instead that B marries C before A commits a felony, a different result obtains. The state of the title after B's marriage: A has a life estate, B has a vested remainder in fee simple, O has nothing. Then A commits a felony. The state of the title is now: B has a fee simple absolute.

Of course, forfeiture is not a concept that was received, at least on a long-term basis, in the course of the American reception of English common law. However, as we have noted earlier, a valid gift requires the beneficiary's acceptance, and any beneficiary of a gift may "renounce" or refuse to accept his or her interest in that gift. A voluntary renunciation may result in the destruction of a contingent remainder as did the involuntary common law forfeiture. For example:

Example 10

O → A for life, then to B and his heirs if B reaches 21.

Or, graphically:

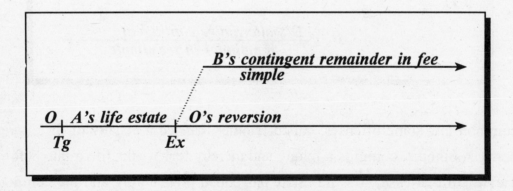

Suppose A decides to decline, or renounce, his or her life interest. (Perhaps, for tax reasons, A does not want the extra income the life estate would generate.) At common law, such a decision jeopardizes B's interest, if B is not yet 21. If A's interest ends prematurely by renunciation, then B's interest will be treated as destroyed by failing to vest in time. O's interest will become possessory. O has a fee simple. (You can see that in declining the gift, A may have non-tax motives.)

B. Gifts to a Class and Vested Remainders, Subject to Open

The family of remainders includes one subspecies of vested remainder that requires a further word of definition. Suppose:

Example 11

O → A for life, then to A's children and their heirs.

Suppose, further, that A has no children. The graphical representation for such a conveyance on this state of facts would be:

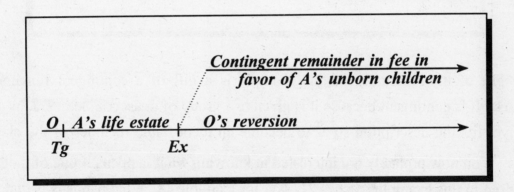

The gift to the class of children of A is a contingent remainder because there is no person who meets the description of the beneficiary to whom the remainder belongs. There is as yet no member of the class of children.

There is nothing unusual about a contingent remainder to a class; it is like a contingent remainder to an individual in that it is destructible and inalienable inter vivos. Take one further example. Suppose:

Example 12

*O → A for life, then to the children of A who reach 21
and their heirs.*

Suppose A has two children, aged 6 and 10. The symbolical representation would be:

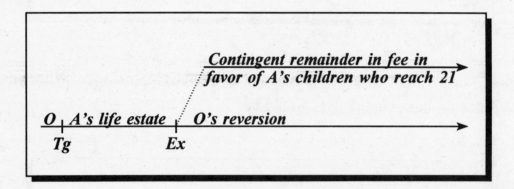

The gift of the remainder in this example is a gift of a contingent remainder interest. It is contingent because it is given to a group of unascertained persons. No one yet fits the description so as to become an identifiable member of the class.

You now probably are interested in knowing what happens if one of the two children in this example reaches 21, say, for example, X. What happens is that the entire remainder is reclassified as vested. Thus, upon a child of A reaching 21, the graphical representation is:

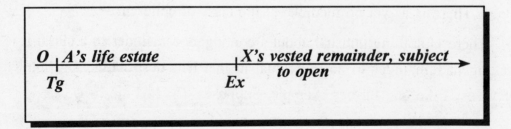

The phrase "subject to open" that appears in the diagram identifies a subspecies of vested remainder—a conveyance to a class of which at least one member is in existence or has met the condition precedent imposed on the class. This species of vested remainder is, like other vested remainders, indestructible; it is alienable inter vivos, devisable and inheritable. It is "subject to open" because for some period of time, the class is open, can increase in number, and X's share might diminish in size.

Suppose, now, in our continuing example, that X's sibling also reaches 21. X and Y share a vested remainder, subject to open, in fee. Suppose X dies, leaving a will in favor of his wife, W. W and Y will share the vested remainder, subject to open, in fee. If X died without a will, a state statute would provide the governing rules for determining successors to X's property, including his share in the vested remainder, subject to open.

Some additional examples of gifts to a class may be useful review and clarification. Suppose:

Example 13

O → A for life, then to the children of A and their heirs.

If A has no children, the state of the title is: A has a life estate, there is a contingent remainder in favor of the children of A, and O has a reversion. We do not call the contingent remainder subject to open.

If, in the above example, O conveys his or her reversion to A, A will have, by the miracle of merger, a fee simple absolute. The contingent remainder in the children of A will be destroyed by failing to vest before the termination of the prior estate, in this case by merger.

If, on the other hand, a child is born to A, the state of the title becomes: A has a life estate, and the child of A now in being has a vested remainder, subject to open, in fee. The reversion is destroyed. The remainder, subject to open, is not destructible. If the child dies leaving a will that favors the child's spouse, the state of the title will be: A has a life estate, and the child's spouse has the vested remainder, subject to open.

There are other important aspects of gifts to a class, such as determining when a class gift closes. A class closes, for example, when the parent whose children are the beneficiaries of a class gift dies. For example, suppose O conveys "*to A for life, remainder to B's children and their heirs*", and on the date of the conveyance O, A and B are living, and B has one child. The state of the title is: A has a life estate, and B's child has a vested remainder, subject to open. Now suppose B dies, survived by his child and by A. The state of the title is: A has a life estate, and B's child has a vested remainder. Since the class has closed, B's child's remainder is no longer "subject to open."

For a further example, suppose O conveys "*to A for life, remainder to B's children and their heirs.*" You might wonder now whether the gift remains open beyond A's death, if B survives A, in order to include children born to B thereafter. The common law evolved something complex but simply stated called "the rule of convenience." This rule in the above example, absent a showing of intent to the contrary, would close the class at the end of A's life estate if any children have been born to B. No children born to B after that point would share. The rule of convenience closes a class as soon as a member of that class is entitled to demand distribution of his or her share. In this example, if a child of B has been born to B before A dies, then that child will be entitled to possession when A dies. This fact will close the class at A's death, unless O has expressed a different intent in the document that created the interests.

It will not surprise you that class gifts involve other legal issues. You will encounter some of them in your course work in property, others in wills and trusts courses and practice, and others in tax courses. This chapter was intended only to provide an introductory understanding of the family of remainders. The following summary and the problems in the review set will give you a chance to practice the new insights.

C.   Summary of Remainders

1.   Vested Remainders (pre-1536)

a.   Vested

Definition: A remainder created in an identifiable grantee or identifiable group that is not subject to any condition and that is not subject to decrease or increase.

Here, and with all remainders, remember to check first to see that the future interest *is* a remainder; i.e., it follows an expirable estate, it is ready to take effect on expiration of the preceding estate and it does not take effect before expiration of the preceding estate.

Examples

vested.

O → A for life, then to B and his heirs.

vested

O → A for life, remainder to B for life.

vested

O → A for life, then to B and his heirs as long as the land is farmed.

In all of the above examples, in the classic common law language of estates in land, B is deemed to have a vested remainder. Notice in example 2 that if B dies before A, B's interest disappears. That, however, is a function of the kind of present estate he or she will have. Further, it is true that in the third example B has an interest that, once it becomes possessory, might be lost on breach of condition. Again, this is a function of the kind of present estate the future interest will become, not a function of the kind of remainder B has been given.

Attributes: Alienable, devisable, inheritable.

b.   Vested, Subject to Open

Definition: A vested remainder belonging to a class of persons that may increase in number.

Examples

$O \rightarrow$ *A for life, then to the children of A and their heirs.* (A has one child, B.)

$O \rightarrow$ *A for life, then to the children of C and their heirs.* (C has one child, B.)

$O \rightarrow$ *A for life, then to B and his children.*

In all three examples, B has a vested remainder, subject to open.

Attributes: Alienable, devisable, inheritable.

2.　Contingent Remainders

Definition: A remainder that is subject to a condition precedent or created in an unborn or unascertainable person.

Examples

O → A for life, then to B and his heirs if B marries C.
　　(Assume that B has not married C.)

O → A for life, remainder to the firstborn son of A and his heirs. (A has no sons.)

O → A for life, then to B's heir. (B is living.)

In all of the above three cases, the remainder is contingent. In the first example, B has a contingent remainder in fee; in the second example, there is a contingent remainder in fee in favor of A's firstborn son; and in the third example, there is a contingent remainder in fee in favor of that person who, on B's death, would be entitled to take any property not devised by will.

Attributes: Destructible by failure to vest before expiration of the preceding estate. Failure to vest may occur in a number of ways. It may happen if the condition precedent becomes impossible to perform. It may occur by merger, or by termination of the prior estate before expiration. Inalienable inter vivos, but devisable and inheritable unless the condition that makes the interest a contingent remainder requires survivorship. Then, of course, the interest would not be devisable or inheritable until the condition requiring survivorship had been met.

D.   Review Problem Set (1500)

Please give the state of the title in each of the following. Assume that O has a fee simple absolute prior to the conveyance. You must give the state of the title for each of the separate fact situations. All fact patterns are to be treated cumulatively.

1.   *O → W for life, then to A and his heirs if A survives W, and if A fails to survive W, then to B and his heirs.*

    a.   O, W, A, and B are all living.

          O reversion
          W - life estate
          A - contingent remainder in fee if A survives W
          B - alternative contingent remainder in fee if A fails to survive W.

    b.   B dies leaving a sole heir, D.

          B - alternative contingent remainder entitled by conveyance of descent

    c.   W dies.

          If A is Alive - fee simple, Destroys B contingent remainder

    d.   A dies leaving a sole heir, E.

          IF A predeceases W   E gets nothing. cannot devise contingent remainder
                        B is fee simple
          IF AFTER W = E fee simple Absolute

2.   *O → A and the heirs of his body, then to the firstborn son of B and his heirs.*

    a.   O, A, and B are all living; neither A nor B has children. A and B are both married.

          O nothing
          A fee tail

    b.   A has a son, C. A's wife dies in childbirth.

c. B has a son, D.

d. B dies.

No effect

e. A dies never having married again and with a will leaving all his property to E and his heirs.

Reverts to O

3. *O → A for life, remainder to the children of A who survive A and their heirs.*

a. A is living but has no children. A is married.

A life estate   contingent remainder to children living cut as death
O reversion

b. A has a child, X.

contingent remainder subject to open
X - Whole ___ expectancy

c. A has a child, Y.

contingent remainder subject to open
X + Y ½ each expectancy

d. X dies, leaving H as an heir.

Contingent remainder, Y who expectancy

e. A dies.

Contingent remainder open = closed
A⁵ all children who survive A share equally

4.   *O → A for life, then to B and his heirs so long as liquor is not sold on the premises.*

   a.   O, A, and B are living.

   O - reverter
   A - life estate
   B - vested remainder in fee determinable

   b.   A dies.

   B fee determinable
   O reverter

   c.   O dies leaving as his heir D.

   D takes reverter

   d.   B opens a liquor store on Blackacre.

   D owns Blackacre — revert to D because condition
   fee simple absolute
   of fee breached

Answers to Review Problem Set

Please give the state of the title in each of the following. Assume that O has a fee simple absolute prior to the conveyance. You must give the state of the title for each of the separate fact situations. All fact patterns are to be treated cumulatively.

1.   *O → W for life, then to A and his heirs if A survives W, and if A fails to survive W, then to B and his heirs.*

    a.   O, W, A, and B are all living.

        W—life estate
        A—contingent remainder in fee simple
        B—alternative contingent remainder in fee simple
        O—reversion

    b.   B dies leaving a sole heir, D.

        No change except D has B's alternative contingent remainder in fee.

> *Note the difference had the problem said "A dies leaving a sole heir, D." While in theory A's contingent remainder is as inheritable as B's, the condition here requires A to survive W. Hence, if A predeceases W, the contingent remainder is destroyed and B's vested remainder follows W's life estate. O's reversion would disappear.*

    c.   W dies.
        A—fee simple absolute.

    d.   A dies leaving a sole heir, E.
        E—fee simple absolute.

2.   *O → A and the heirs of his body, then to the firstborn son of B and his heirs.*

   a.   O, A, and B are all living; neither A nor B have children. A and B are both married.

   A—fee tail.
   Firstborn son of B—contingent remainder in fee simple.
   O—reversion.

   b.   A has a son, C. A's wife dies in childbirth.

   No change.

   c.   B has a son, D.

   A—fee tail.
   D—vested remainder in fee simple.

   d.   B dies.

   No change.

   e.   A dies never having married again, and with a will leaving all his property to E and his heirs.

   C—fee tail.
   D—vested remainder in fee simple.
   E—nothing.

3.   *O → A for life, remainder to the children of A who survive A and their heirs.*

   a.   A is living but has no children.

   A—life estate.
   There is a contingent remainder in favor of the children of A who survive A.
   O—reversion.

b.   A has a child, X.

No change.

c.   A has a child, Y.

No change.

d.   X dies, leaving H as an heir.

No change. H inherits nothing.

e.   A dies.

Y—fee simple absolute.

4.   *O → A for life, then to B and his heirs so long as liquor is not sold on the premises.*

a.   O, A, and B are living.

O—possibility of reverter.
A—life estate.
B—vested remainder in fee simple determinable.

b.   A dies.

O—possibility of reverter.
B—fee simple determinable.

c.   O dies leaving as his heir D.

No change except D has O's possibility of reverter.

d.   B opens a liquor store on Blackacre.

D—fee simple absolute.

CHAPTER FOUR

PRESENT AND FUTURE INTERESTS AFTER 1536

A. Executory Interests and the Fee Simple on Executory Limitation

Look again at problem 3(c) in the Problem Set at the end of Chapter Two. O wants A to have a fee simple—"almost"; i.e., she wants the land to go to her friend B, if B returns from Rome. You should have decided that before 1536, O could not accomplish that desire. That was true in the common law courts. We will continue to be concerned only with legal estates in land (as opposed not to "illegal estates" but to "equitable interests"—the distinction shortly shall become clearer). However, in order to explain how O might accomplish her wish, we must turn our attention for a moment to the Court of Equity and to a legislative change in 1536.

In the period between 1066 and 1536, the world of the common law and the profession practiced by the common law lawyers had expanded greatly. During this period of approximately five hundred years, the important common law courts had emerged, Parliament had become an important representative body that initiated significant legislation, and the body of common law principles had proliferated. From relatively simple beginnings, the forms of action had evolved to enable the common law courts to entertain more kinds of complaints and thus to award damages for more types of injuries.

At the same time, the procedural aspects of the forms of action, including the pleading stage (perhaps particularly the pleading stage), had become increasingly technical and slow. Further, the forms of action, even as multiple and flexible as they were, did not afford universal justice.

In response to the gaps and disadvantages of the common law legal process, an alternative channel of justice widened. During the very same five-hundred-year period that produced the common law courts, Parliament, common law pleading, and an enlarged number of common law forms of action, that officer of the King's household called the Chancellor increasingly became a source of relief not otherwise available. On behalf of the King, this household officer exercised a delegated authority to order compensation, decree specific performance, and otherwise compel activity that to him seemed just or "equitable."

The petitions directed to the Chancellor probably at first represented unique problems. Later, many petitions fell into a few categories as the Chancellor's expertise became more specialized. One of the most important categories seems to have been petitions with respect to conveyances of real property. These petitions asked that the Chancellor intervene in order to mitigate the hardship of results that obtained at common law.

Take, for example, Review Problem 3(c) at the end of Chapter Two:

> *O → A and his heirs,* **but if B returns from Rome then to B and his heirs**.

As you know, O's interest was not possible to be carried out at common law. B's interest does not satisfy the definition of a remainder, and there was no other common law possibility. In the common law courts, the emphasized words were apparently void. A was treated as having a fee simple; the balance of the conveyance was simply meaningless surplusage at common law.

Yet, O could have constructed a conveyance that the Chancellor would have enforced to accomplish his desire. O could have created a *use*:[*]

---

[*]Not everyone sees the recognition of the use as an historical event worthy of celebration. *See, e.g.,* G. Thompson, *Commentaries on the Modern Law of Real Property* § 4290, at 223 (J. Grimes ed., 1963):

> But about the middle of the thirteenth century the "use" slithered into this Garden of Eden. Thus there developed a party whose rights in the land were not always visible since he might not be in open possession but which rights were protected by the equity courts. Uses apparently were not usually shown even on the manorial roles. Indeed secrecy was one of the major areas of usefulness.

> *Legal Title*　　　*Equitable Title*
>
> $O \rightarrow T$ *and his heirs, for the use of A and his heirs, but if B ever returns from Rome, then for the use of B and his heirs.*

This grant contains only one conveyance that the common law courts recognized: O has conveyed a fee simple absolute to T; T has the *legal* title to Blackacre. The Chancellor would require, however, that T honor any promise he had made to manage the estate for the benefit of A and, if the condition was met, for the benefit of B. Process in the Chancellor's court, the Court of Chancery, began with a petition. Discovery mechanisms, such as depositions and interrogatories, were available. A nonjury trial before the Chancellor followed. Eventually, if the Chancellor decided affirmatively for A and B, a decree would issue, perhaps in the form of injunctive relief.

The process, the principles, and the remedies were all sufficiently different from those available in the common law courts that the words "equitable rights" and "equitable relief" began to be used to describe them. It was appropriate, for example, to describe A and B as having equitable rights as a result of the conveyance to T. T was said to have the legal interest; A and B had equitable interests. For reasons that are not altogether clear, the Chancellor was willing to enforce equitable future interests in a grantee that did not satisfy the common law conveyancing rules. His willingness to recognize future interests in grantees that did not satisfy the common law rules relative to remainders greatly added to the Chancellor's jurisdiction and power. There were advantages to the use other than the avoidance of common law conveyancing rules. The use became a popular tax-avoidance device, for example. Further, the use permitted owners of interests in land to devise such interests long before the Statute of Wills was enacted in 1540.

In 1536, Parliament passed the Statute of Uses, 27 Hen. VIII, Ch. 10. The Statute gave legal status to interests that, before then, were only enforceable in equity through the use. The Statute of Uses, you will be glad to know, did not make illegal or change the treatment of any of the present or future interests you have already mastered. Rather, as a result of the Statute, some interests that until then had been recognized only in equity gained protection in the courts that applied the common law. This allowed the common law courts to recapture lost judicial business at the jurisdictional expense of the court of equity.

As a result of the Statute of Uses, the list of common law estates in land was expanded to include one new present interest and one new future interest. The new present interest is the fee simple on executory limitation. The new future interest is called an executory interest. The relationship between these new estates is really quite like that between the old fee simple determinable and the possibility of reverter, the difference being that the executory interest is a future interest in a **grantee** while, as you know, a possibility of reverter was always in the **grantor**. The similarity leads us to diagram the two conveyances very much alike:

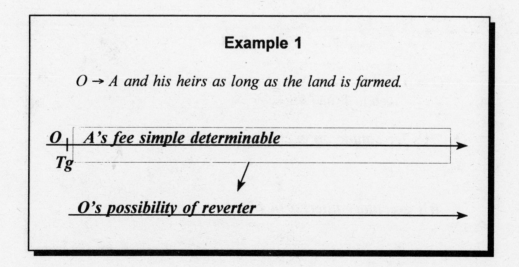

Example 1

O → A and his heirs as long as the land is farmed.

O | *A's fee simple determinable*

Tg

O's possibility of reverter

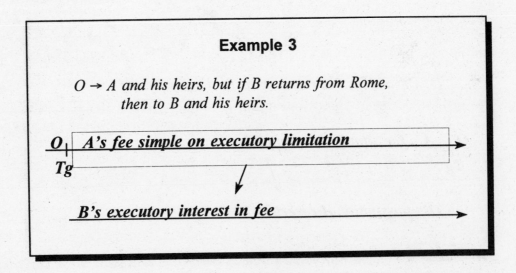

The fee simple on executory limitation was alienable, inheritable, and devisable (after the Statute of Wills in 1540) at common law. The executory interest was inheritable and devisable (after 1540), but was originally inalienable by gift or sale at the common law.

Here are some more examples of the "new" estates:

Hence, you see, the grantor's wish in Chapter Two, Problem 3(c) can now be met.

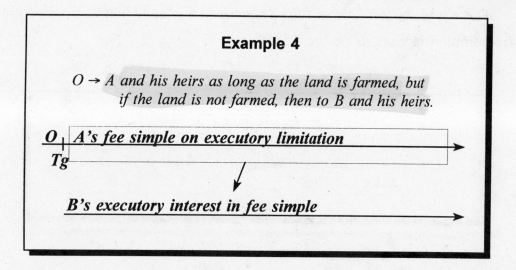

This example presents a bit of a problem. You should know, now, to call the future interest B's executory interest in fee simple. But has A's present estate changed? It used to be called a "fee simple determinable," because all the words after "farmed" would have been disregarded before 1536 as violative of the common law conveyancing rules. Should we continue to call it a fee simple determinable now that the Statute of Uses allows the gift over to B? Or should we call it a fee simple on executory limitation, the new present possessory estate, because it is now followed by an executory interest? We think that, for this initial presentation, it doesn't matter very much, and we're going to rename it. Not all experts in this field would agree with that; there are certainly cases that describe A's interest in Example 4 as a "fee simple determinable." Your Property teacher, in fact, may think it is an important distinction. (We urge you to pay attention to your teacher in such matters.) But we're going to call A's interest a fee simple on executory limitation, followed by B's executory interest in fee. That result has the attraction of keeping the two new estates related and furthermore leaves intact what you learned above: a fee simple determinable is always followed by a possibility of reverter.

There was another kind of future interest in a grantee that was not permitted by the common law courts before 1536:

Example 5

O → A for life, then one year after A's death, to B and his heirs.

The future interest in B was too patient for the common law courts to tolerate. Recall that prior to 1536 a future interest in a grantee had to be ready to take *immediately* on the expiration of the preceding life estate. At the common law, Example 5 would have resulted in a life estate in A and a reversion in O.

After 1536, a conveyance like Example 5 became legal:

O | *A's life estate* | *O's reversion* | *B's executory interest in fee* →
Tg   Ex   Ex+1

A has a life estate and B has an executory interest in fee. O takes the property during the one-year hiatus; O has a reversion, which you will notice is subject to an executory interest. When the reversion becomes possessory, the present estate will be a fee simple on executory limitation.

Note, too, that we can now have a conveyance that creates no new possessory estate at all:

Example 6

O → B and his heirs upon his marriage.

B's interest is entirely future and would have been prohibited prior to 1536. After the Statute of Uses, B has an executory interest in fee. O retains the present estate and it is called a fee simple on executory limitation.

Look back over the six examples given above. Note that in some of them—Nos. 2, 3 and 4—the possession of the property, if it changes at all, will go from A to B. In some of them—Nos. 5 and 6—the possession will go from O to B. The first kind of executory interest is called "shifting" and the second kind is called "springing." This is not a very important distinction and little if anything—other than perhaps your exam score—depends on the classification anymore. But the terms are still used and you should get to know them. In case you'd like more formal definitions, here they are:

(a)   *Shifting* executory interests are those that, before 1536, would have failed because they attempted to cut short the prior estate and to take effect before the expiration of the preceding life estate or fee tail.

(b)   *Springing* executory interests are those that, prior to 1536, would have failed because they were written to take effect at a time subsequent to the expiration of the preceding estate.

It is an important fact that the Statute of Uses added new interests to an existing system; the inventory of estates in land and future interests increased, as we have seen so far, by the addition of fees on executory limitation and executory interests. (It is more than just possible that the ultimate impact of this result was not fully anticipated by those early legislators. If so, they are not without counterparts in modern times, and there are other things they likely did not foresee.)

But the Statute left intact all the estates that had been valid before 1536. So, there's some good news here: all that you learned about the five present and five future interests in the first three chapters remains true for a few hundred more years—two more chapters. The Statute recognized a new present estate and a new future interest, but it truly only puts an "overlay" of an executory regime onto the existing system.

That regime includes a refinement of the reversion as seen above, as well as a refinement of the vested remainder, which we now explain. Consider the following example:

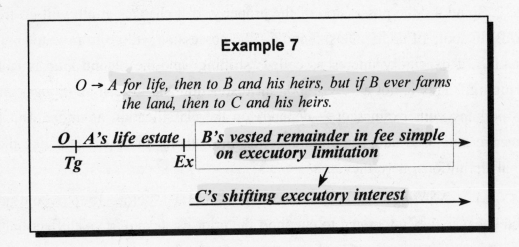

Example 7

O → A for life, then to B and his heirs, but if B ever farms the land, then to C and his heirs.

O ⏐ A's life estate ⏐ B's vested remainder in fee simple on executory limitation →
Tg ⏐ Ex ↓
C's shifting executory interest →

Example 7 is really not very new. It merely involves your old task of identifying what interest B will have when his interest becomes possessory. Here, B's present interest will be a fee simple on executory limitation. B's remainder is vested because there is no condition precedent and B is born and ascertainable. B (or someone who succeeds to B's interest) is certain to come into possession of Blackacre; however, B may lose it to C if B does not possess it according to the condition. After the Statute of Uses recognized executory interests, O was able to create such interests as B's vested remainder in fee simple on executory limitation.

Now, try another example.

Example 8

O → A for life, then to B and his heirs, but if A ever farms the land, then to C and his heirs.

What is the state of the title? Well, A has a life estate. B's remainder looks vested by your usual tests: B is born and ascertainable and there is no condition precedent. But, wait a minute.

The "but if ..." clause is a condition subsequent. The definition of a vested remainder evolved well before the Statute of Uses, and the language associated with a condition precedent ("if ...") and a condition subsequent ("but if ...") probably became standard language relatively early. The Statute of Uses, as you know, changed none of the remainder rules. Hence, the recognition of the legitimacy of a condition subsequent did not, in itself, make a remainder, subject to a condition subsequent, contingent.

So, you conclude, B has a vested remainder before 1536, and so he does even after 1536. Remember that the Statute of Uses only recognized new interests; it didn't change old interests. After the Statute of Uses, however, a remainder, although vested, may be "divested" before it ever becomes possessory. B, in our example, has such a remainder: a vested remainder, subject to divestment. If B's interest ever becomes possessory, that is, if it avoids divestment while a remainder, then B will hold in fee simple; thus, the complete name for B's future interest is a vested remainder, subject to divestment, in fee simple. C has a shifting executory interest in fee.

So far our classification scheme is rather tidy: B has a vested remainder subject to divestment in fee if he will lose his remainder while it is still a remainder, and a vested remainder in fee simple on executory limitation if he will lose his interest after it becomes possessory. Suppose B could lose the interest either while it is a remainder or after it becomes possessory? Suppose:

Example 9

O → A for life, then to B and his heirs, but if B dies under 21, then to C and his heirs.

B, of course, could die younger than 21 either during A's life, thereby divesting the remainder, or after A's death, thereby removing B from possession. From what you have learned from the two previous examples you might choose to call B's interest a vested remainder, subject to divestment, in fee simple on executory limitation. You may call it that, if your elocution is up to it. It is more typical to call it a vested remainder, subject to divestment, in fee. In other words, the standard classification scheme limits its description of the interest represented by a vested remainder, subject to divestment. (You might now compare O's interest in Example 5. There, too, it is typical to limit the description of the future interest. Thus, in that example, we described O as having a reversion.)

Look again at Example 9 and suppose that B dies at 19. The remainder is destroyed for sure, but does A lose possession? If O wanted A to lose possession on B's untimely death, the present estate would be called a **life estate on executory limitation.** *As you will see in Chapter Six, that was permitted after 1536, but it had to be done* **very** *clearly. The grant in Example 9 is not clear enough. A has a life estate.*

The above examples illustrate the fact that, after executory interests are recognized, we have a further refinement to the vested remainder: vested, subject to divestment. A vested remainder, subject to divestment, is a vested remainder that is subject to an executory interest.

There you have it. This chapter has described certain changes made in 1536, and when you have mastered these changes you have mastered the basic common law system of estates in land and future interests. Good job! You have learned six basic present interests and six basic future interests. OK, it is true that a vested remainder, one of the six future interests, has at least three facets:

(1)   it can be vested indefeasibly, that is, in an identifiable person, without condition precedent and without being subject to an executory interest or a condition subsequent;

(2)   it can be vested, subject to open; or

(3)   after the Statute of Uses it can be vested, subject to divestment, that is, vested, but subject to an executory interest. Review Problem 4 in the problem set at the end of this chapter explores this concept in more detail.

In later chapters we will introduce you to some complexities and show you some cases and statutes that changed the basic system, but for now, you have learned the basic concepts and vocabulary. Take a look at the review charts. Test your knowledge with the problem set.

B.   Review Materials

On the next two pages you will find two charts summarizing the information that you have learned to this point. Both charts may be used for review. You might also use the first chart to try creating the various interests described. For example, can you write a grant that creates a shifting executory interest in fee simple determinable? Use the second chart to decide whether such an interest is alienable.

PRESENT AND FUTURE INTERESTS CREATED OUT OF A FEE SIMPLE ABSOLUTE IN LAND (1700)		
PRESENT INTEREST	**POSSIBLE FUTURE INTERESTS**	
Created in Transferee	**In Transferor or His Estate**	**In Transferee(s)**
Fee Simple Absolute	None	None
Fee Tail	Reversion	Vested Remainder *e.g.*, in fee simple ... no further interest in fee simple on executory limitation ... executory interest in subsequent transferee in life estate ... reversion Contingent Remainder *e.g.*, in fee simple ... reversion in fee simple ... alternative contingent remainder ... reversion Executory Interest *e.g.*, in fee simple ... no further interest
Life Estate	Reversion	Same as for Fee Tail
Fee Simple Determinable	Possibility of Reverter	None
Fee Simple Subject to Condition Subsequent	Right of Entry (Power of Termination)	None
Fee Simple on Executory Limitation	Depends on type of executory interest created	Executory Interest *e.g.*, in fee simple ... no further interest in life estate ... reversion in grantor

SUMMARY OF TRANSFERABILITY (1700)			
Present Interests	**Alienable Inter Vivos**	**Devisable**	**Inheritable**
Fee Simple Absolute	Yes	Yes	Yes
Fee Tail	Limited	No	Modified
Life Estate	Yes	No	No
Fee Simple Determinable	Yes	Yes	Yes
Fee Simple on Condition Subsequent	Yes	Yes	Yes
Fee Simple on Executory Limitation	Yes	Yes	Yes
Future Interests			
Reversion	Yes	Yes	Yes
Possibility of Reverter	No	No*	Yes
Right of Entry	No	No	Yes
Remainder: Vested	Yes	Yes	Yes
Contingent	No	Yes	Yes
Executory Interest	No	Yes	Yes

*The answer here depends on an interpretation of the original English Statute of Wills (1540), as amended in 1542. The Statute provided for the devise of estates "in possession, reversion or remainder." There is some authority that possibilities of reverter, like rights of entry, were not within the 1542 amendment. Other authorities are not satisfied this is so. See L. Simes & A. Smith, **The Law of Future Interests** § 1901, at 200 (2d ed. 1956).*

C. Review Problem Set

1. Give the "state of the title" in each of the grants below, that is to say, tell what present or future interest in the land each of the parties has at the time of the grant, 1591.

   a. *O → A and his heirs, but if B should return from Rome, to B and his heirs.* [O, A, and B are living. B is in Rome.]

   O has _nothing_

   A has _fee simple on Executory limitation_

   B has _shifting executory interest in fee_

   b. *O → A and his heirs, but if A should marry B, to C and his heirs.* [O, A, B, and C are living. A is unmarried.]

   O has _nothing_

   A has _fee simple on executory limitation_

   B has _nothing_

   C has _shifting executory interest in fee_

c. *O → A for life, and one year after A's death, to B and his heirs.* [O, A, and B are living.]

O has _reversion *if fee simple* subject to executory interest_

A has _Life estate_

B has _springing executory interest in fee_

d. *O → A and his heirs upon A's marriage.* [O and A are living. A is unmarried.]

O has _fee simple on Executory limitation_

A has _springing executory interest in fee_

e. *O → A for life, then to B and his heirs, but if B dies under 21, then to C and his heirs.*
[O, A, B, and C are living. B is 19.]

O has _none_

A has _life estate_

B has _vested remainder, subject to divestment, in fee_

C has _shifting executory interest in fee_

2. In each case below, what is B's interest? [**Tg** = 1591.]

a. *O → A and his heirs, but if the land is ever used for commercial purposes, to B and his heirs.*
[B is living. The land is being farmed.]

B shifting executory interest in fee

b. *O → A for life, then to W for life, then if Z is still alive, to C for life, otherwise to B and his heirs.*
[A, W, Z, C, and B are living.]

B has an alternative contingent remainder in fee

c. *O → A for life, then to B and his heirs.* [A and B are living.]

Vested remainder in fee

3. In each case below, O is your client in 1591. If possible, construct a grant that will dispose of his property in the way he desires. If it can't be done, explain why.

a. O wants A to have a fee simple—"almost"; *i.e.*, he never wants the land to be used for commercial purposes, with the additional condition that if the land *is* ever used for commercial purposes, he wants it to go to another friend, C, for that friend's life.

O to A and his heirs, But if the land is ever used for commercial purposes, then to C for life.

b.	O wants his friend A to have the land for A's lifetime and then he wants it to go to his friend B's youngest son, but only if B marries C. If B doesn't marry C, then O wants the land to go to the Church, but only for as long as it is used for Church purposes.

O to A for life, then if B marries C C to B's youngest son and his heirs, But if B does not marry C then to the Catholic Church. Its successors and Assigns for as long as it is used for Church purposes

4.	Give the state of the title; assume the grant is in 1591:

a.	*O → A for life, then if B survives A, to B and his heirs, but if B does not survive A, then to C and his heirs.*
	[A, B, and C are living.]

O has ___*reversion	why?*___

A has ___*life estate*___

B has ___*vested remainder, subject to divestment, in fee*___

C has ___*shifting executory interest.*___

b.	*O → A for life, then to B and his heirs, but if A joins the Church, then upon A's death to the Church, its successors and assigns.* [A and B are living. A is not a member of the Church.]

A has ___*life estate*___

B has _vested remainder, subject to divestment in fee_

Church has _shifting executory_ interest in fee simple subject to ex. limitation

c.   *O → A for life, then to B and his heirs, but if B uses the land*
     for commercial purposes, then to C and his heirs.
     [A, B, and C are living.]

A has _life estate_

B has _vested remainder_ in fee simple on Executory limitation

C has _shifting executory interest in fee_

d.   *O → A for life, then to B and his heirs, but if B joins the*
     Church, then upon A's death to the Church forever.
     [A and B are living. B is not a member of the Church.]

A has _life estate_

B has _vested remainder, subject to divestment, in fee_ ~~~~~~~~~~

Church has _shifting executory interest in fee_

     alternative e

e.   *O → A for life, then to B and his heirs, but if B does not survive A, then to C and his heirs.*
[A, B, and C are living.]

O has _reversion_

B has _vested remainder, subject to divestment, in fee,_

C has _shifting executory interest in fee_

5.   Give the state of the title; assume in both cases that A and B are living and that A is farming the land:

a.   *O → A and her heirs, but if the land ceases to be farmed by A, then to B and his heirs.*

A has _fee simple on executory limitation_

B has _shifting executory interest in fee_

b.   *O → A and her heirs as long as the land is farmed by A, then to B and his heirs.*

A has _fee simple on executory limitation_

B has _shifting executory interest in fee_

Answers to Review Problem Set

1. Give the "state of the title" in each of the grants below, that is to say, tell what present or future interest in the land each of the parties has at the time of the grant, 1591.

    a. *O → A and his heirs, but if B should return from Rome, to B and his heirs.* [O, A, and B are living. B is in Rome.]

    O has nothing.
    A has a fee simple on executory limitation.
    B has a shifting executory interest in fee simple.

    b. *O → A and his heirs, but if A should marry B, to C and his heirs.* [O, A, B, and C are living. A is unmarried.]

    O has nothing.
    A has a fee simple on executory limitation.
    B has nothing. (Don't worry about what entitlements B might have as A's spouse.)
    C has a shifting executory interest in fee simple.

    c. *O → A for life, and one year after A's death, to B and his heirs.* [O, A, and B are living.]

    O has a reversion (in fee simple on executory limitation).
    A has a life estate.
    B has a springing executory interest in fee simple.

    > The material in parentheses is frequently omitted.

    d. *O → A and his heirs upon A's marriage.* [O and A are living. A is unmarried.]

    O has a fee simple on executory limitation.
    A has a springing executory interest in fee simple.

e. *O → A for life, then to B and his heirs, but if B dies under 21, then to C and his heirs.* [O, A, B, and C are living. B is 19.]

O has nothing.
A has a life estate.
B has a vested remainder, subject to divestment, in fee.
C has a shifting executory interest in fee simple.

2. In each case below, what is B's interest? [*Tg* = 1591.]

a. *O → A and his heirs, but if the land is ever used for commercial purposes, to B and his heirs.*
[B is living. The land is being farmed.]

B has a shifting executory interest in fee simple.

b. *O → A for life, then to W for life, then if Z is still alive, to C for life, otherwise to B and his heirs.* [A, W, Z, C, and B are living.]

B has an alternative contingent remainder in fee simple.

c. *O → A for life, then to B and his heirs.* [A and B are living.]

B has a vested remainder in fee simple.

3. In each case below, O is your client in 1591. If possible, construct a grant that will dispose of his property in the way he desires. If it can't be done, explain why.

a. O wants A to have a fee simple—"almost"; *i.e.*, he never wants the land to be used for commercial purposes, with the additional condition that if the land *is* ever used for commercial purposes, he wants it to go to another friend, C, for that friend's life.

O → A and his heirs, but if the land is ever used for commercial purposes, then to C.

b. O wants his friend A to have the land for A's lifetime and then he wants it to go to his friend B's youngest son, but only if B marries C. If B doesn't marry C, then O wants the land to go to the Church, but only for as long as it is used for Church purposes.

O → A for life, then if B marries C, to B's youngest son and his heirs, otherwise to the Church as long as it is used for Church purposes.

4.   Give the state of the title; assume the time of the grant is 1591.

a.   *O → A for life, then if B survives A, to B and his heirs, but if B does not survive A, then to C and his heirs.*
[A, B, and C are living.]

A has a life estate.
B and C have alternative contingent remainders.
O has a reversion.

b.   *O → A for life, then to B and his heirs, but if A joins the Church, then upon A's death to the Church, its successors and assigns.*
[A and B are living. A is not a member of the Church.]

A has a life estate.
B has a vested remainder, subject to divestment, in fee.
The Church has a shifting executory interest in fee.

c.   *O → A for life, then to B and his heirs, but if B uses the land for commercial purposes, then to C and his heirs.*
[A, B, and C are living.]

A has a life estate.
B has a vested remainder in fee simple on executory limitation.
C has a shifting executory interest in fee.

d.   *O → A for life, then to B and his heirs, but if B joins the Church, then upon A's death to the Church forever.*
[A and B are living. B is not a member of the Church.]

A has a life estate.
B has a vested remainder, subject to divestment, in fee.
The Church has a shifting executory interest in fee.

e.   *O → A for life, then to B and his heirs, but if B does not survive A, then to C and his heirs.* [A, B, and C are living.]

A has a life estate.
B has a vested remainder, subject to divestment, in fee.
C has a shifting executory interest in fee.

The difficulty is to explain why the answer to (e) is not exactly the same as the answer to (a). It isn't, and the easy explanation—the phrase "if B survives A" is missing—is somewhat unsatisfactory. The other grants may help explain the difference between (a) and (e), but the difference is a subtle one and we've put the explanation here in the Problem Set instead of the text to indicate that we consider it "advanced learning."

Reread the "but if" clause in (b), (c) and (d). You will note that in (b) the condition will be broken, if ever, during A's lifetime—A cannot join the Church after he is dead. The condition in (c), on the other hand, will be broken, if ever, only after A's death, when B comes into possession and begins to use the land. Finally, in (d), the condition may be broken either during A's life, or after his death.

*In each of (b), (c) and (d), B has a vested remainder because he is ready to take the property on A's death and there is no condition precedent to his taking. You might want to say that in (b) there **is** a condition precedent—that A not join the Church—but the common law considered the condition contained in a "but if" clause a condition subsequent. We call B's interest in (b) a vested remainder, subject to divestment, in fee because the remainder may be lost through breach of condition during the period of time it is a future interest. B's interest in (c) is a vested remainder in fee simple on executory limitation. It is not a vested remainder, subject to divestment, because B can lose his fee simple only after he comes into possession. B's interest in (d) might be described by the following mouthful: a vested remainder, subject to divestment, in fee simple on executory limitation. However, as noted earlier, it is typical to describe B's interest as a vested remainder, subject to divestment, in fee.*

Finally, what about (e)? The "but if" condition in this example will be broken, if ever, during A's life (by B's death). Hence, it resembles example (b), and B has a vested remainder, subject to divestment, in fee. The difference between (a) and (e) lies in the legal consequence that the "but if" clause acts as a condition subsequent to divest a vested remainder in (e). In (a), however, the language of the conveyance establishes the first remainder as contingent (subject to a condition precedent); the second remainder is deemed also to be subject to a condition precedent by virtue of following a contingent remainder.

*One final complexity and then you will have it all: look again at (b) and (e), the two instances in which we have just classified B's interest as a vested remainder, subject to divestment, in fee. Suppose A renounces his life estate. B's remainder is vested, so B comes into possession immediately. However, the condition, which before renunciation looked like it would be broken, if ever, **before** B took possession, may now be broken **after** B takes possession, since A is still alive. The condition is still viable and may remove B from possession. That is what we usually call a fee simple on executory limitation, and we ought to describe B's interest following renunciation by A as a fee simple on executory limitation.*

5.   Give the state of the title; assume in both cases that A and B are living and that A is farming the land:

a.   *O → A and her heirs, but if the land ceases to be farmed by A, then to B and his heirs.*

A has a fee simple on executory limitation.
B has a shifting executory interest in fee.

b.   *O → A and her heirs as long as the land is farmed by A, then to B and his heirs.*

A has a fee simple on executory limitation.
B has a shifting executory interest in fee.

> *Here's a point we made above in the text. We will call A's interest in both 5(a) and 5(b) a fee simple on executory limitation for what we think are proper pedagogic reasons. We understand, though, that from the perspective of the cases, 5(b) might more properly give A a fee simple determinable. Take your lead from your Property teacher on this one. We all agree that B's interest in both cases is a shifting executory interest in fee.*

CHAPTER FIVE

LATER MODIFICATIONS OF THE BASIC COMMON LAW SCHEME:
Common Law Responses to the Statute of Uses

You have learned so far many of the concepts and the vocabulary necessary for you to maneuver in the area of estates in land and future interests. You have learned six basic present, possessory estates and six basic future interests. You have also learned that the concept of remainders has several subconcepts: vested; vested, subject to open; vested, subject to divestment; and contingent. (Some writers and courts add another category: "indefeasibly vested," used for emphasis when a divesting condition cannot occur until after the remainder becomes possessory. *See* Problem 4(c) in Chapter Four. We think calling the remainder "vested" is emphatic enough.) You also know that the Statute of Uses led to the executory interest, that the recognition of the executory interest produced a new kind of fee—the fee simple on executory limitation—and that the existence of executory interests also gives us the concept of a vested remainder, subject to divestment.

All the ramifications of the Statute of Uses were not foreseen nor were they necessarily foreseeable. One of the features of the evolution of the common law, at least the common law of property, has been the elaboration of ideas in unforeseen yet functional directions. Professor Rabin has noted that "[m]ost changes in the law create important unanticipated side effects. These side effects are sometimes beneficial and sometimes harmful." E. Rabin, *Fundamentals of Modern Real Property* 22 (1974). (Who would have thought, for example, that the only lasting consequence of the eighteenth amendment to the U.S. Constitution would be the proliferation of organized crime?) Perhaps because it is so old, perhaps because it is remarkably durable, and perhaps because it is so uniquely of common law origin, the law of property especially illustrates the pragmatic and haphazard course of common law evolution. This chapter is designed to describe one part of that story: the response of the common law of real property to the Statute of Uses. First, however, you will need to recall that special attribute of a contingent remainder—destructibility.

A.   The Destructibility of Contingent Remainders: A Review

Contingent remainders led precarious lives. They were destructible in several ways. Examples of the three primary situations that resulted in the destruction of contingent remainders are as follows:

1.   Merger

Merger applies when one person owns a possessory estate or a vested interest (the vested interests are reversions and vested remainders) and the *next* vested interest. Under some circumstances, the lesser of the two interests will be absorbed by the greater. The first example that follows illustrates merger; compare the second example.

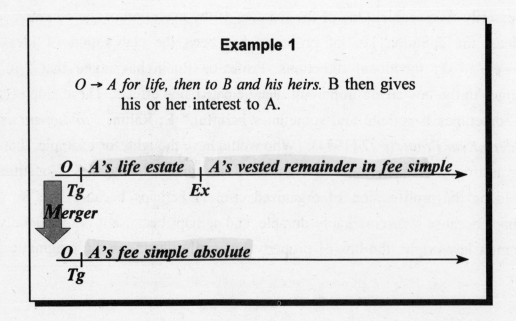

Example 1

$O \rightarrow$ *A for life, then to B and his heirs.* B then gives
his or her interest to A.

O | *A's life estate* | *A's vested remainder in fee simple*
Tg   *Ex*
Merger

O | *A's fee simple absolute*
Tg

Example 2

O → A for life, then to B for life, then to A and his
heirs.

O | A's life estate | B's vested remainder | A's vested remainder
Tg   *Ex*   *for life*   *Ex*   *in fee*

No merger   A does not own the vested interest *next*
after the possessory estate.

Merger can result in the destruction of contingent remainders. For example, when the prior estate on which the contingent remainder is dependent ceases to exist as a result of merging into a larger estate, the dependent contingent remainder is said to have been destroyed.

Example 3

O → A for life, then to the first son of A who reaches 21.
    (A's son S is 15.)

Contingent remainder in favor
of A's first son to reach 21

O | A's life estate | O's reversion
Tg   *Ex*

There is no opportunity for merger here, initially, since A has only the possessory estate. Suppose, however, that O conveys his or her reversion to A (you will recall that reversions are alienable). Now, A owns the possessory estate and the next vested interest, and they merge:

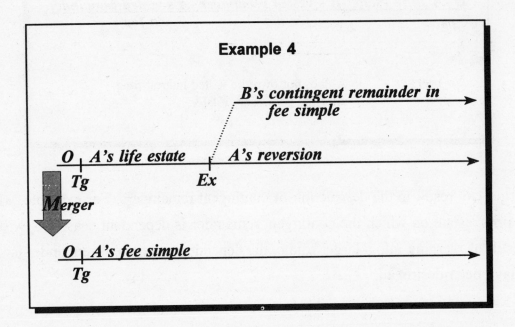

Example 4

B's contingent remainder in fee simple

O | A's life estate   A's reversion
Tg   Ex

Merger

O | A's fee simple
Tg

What about the contingent remainder? It is destroyed. This is one example of the destructibility of contingent remainders—destruction as a consequence of merger.

Merger will not destroy contingent remainders when all the estates involved were created by one grant. Note that in Example 3 above, the contingent remainder was destroyed by O's second conveyance, of his or her reversion, to A. Another example follows.

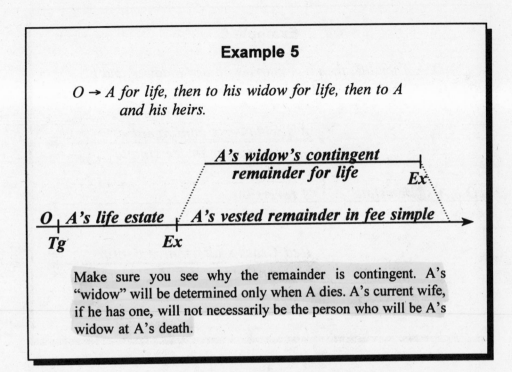

Example 5

*O → A for life, then to his widow for life, then to A
and his heirs.*

Make sure you see why the remainder is contingent. A's
"widow" will be determined only when A dies. A's current wife,
if he has one, will not necessarily be the person who will be A's
widow at A's death.

A owns the possessory estate and the next vested interest, but the estates do not merge to destroy the contingent remainder in A's surviving wife, because all the estates were created with one grant. Note, however, that A may convey a fee simple absolute to B, by selling both his life estate and his vested remainder. Then the requisites of merger are met because the appropriate estates are held by a single person and the situation was not created by a single conveyance.

2.   Forfeiture

Forfeiture of the present estate may also cause contingent remainders to be destroyed.

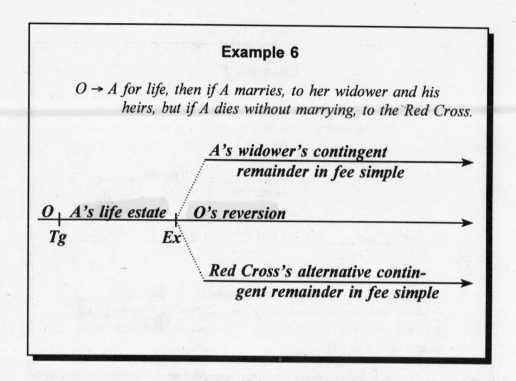

Example 6

O → A for life, then if A marries, to her widower and his heirs, but if A dies without marrying, to the Red Cross.

A's widower's contingent remainder in fee simple

O | A's life estate | O's reversion

Tg | Ex

Red Cross's alternative contingent remainder in fee simple

Now, suppose A renounces her life estate. (At early common law, a similar result obtained if A committed treason or another felony.) The contingencies are not ready to be tested, and hence we cannot choose between the alternate contingent remainders. O's reversion, on the other hand, is vested and O stands ready to take at any time. (What if O is dead? Remember, a reversion is inheritable. O's successors stand ready to take at any time.) The contingent remainders are destroyed and O or O's successors take possession in fee simple. O takes in fee simple because, under the terms of the grant, after the destruction of the contingent remainders, no one else has any interest.

3. Natural Expiration

A contingent remainder also is destroyed if the estate preceding it expires before the remainder becomes vested. This possibility provides frequent opportunities for destruction of contingent remainders.

Example 7

$O \rightarrow A$ for life, then to the first son of A who reaches 21 and his heirs.

Contingent remainder in fee in favor of A's first son to reach 21 →

O | _A's life estate_ | _O's reversion_ →
Tg   Ex

The remainder will stay contingent until one of A's sons reaches 21. If A dies while his oldest son is 19, the contingent remainder is destroyed and O takes his reversion. What happens two years later when the son reaches 21? Nothing. The remainder was destroyed by failing to vest in time.

4.   Summary

Thus, there are three primary instances that illustrate the doctrine of the destructibility of contingent remainders: merger, forfeiture, and natural expiration. True, in many states these days, contingent remainders are not destructible due to statutory removal of the doctrine or judicial abolition. Here, as always, we are talking about the state of the early common law. We ask that you postpone "modern" inquiries until Chapter Seven.

Remember, we are dealing here with the destructibility of **contingent** remainders. Vested remainders are not destructible. Remember, too, that we are dealing here with the destructibility of contingent **remainders**. The same rules do not apply to executory interests or other future interests. This thought is continued in the next section.

B. The Indestructibility of Executory Interests and Related Rules (or *Pells* and *Purefoy*)

Contingent remainders and executory interests are very much alike. For example, both were inalienable inter vivos at common law, but both were devisable and both were inheritable. Further, they are both similar in function.

Example 8

$O \rightarrow A$ for life, remainder to B and his heirs if B marries C.

    B has a contingent remainder in fee.

$O \rightarrow B$ and his heirs if B marries C.

    B has a springing executory interest in fee.

B's interest in both parts of Example 8 is dependent on an event that may or may not occur. It is the "contingency" of each that probably made both interests inalienable at common law.

For reasons that are obscure, the common law courts were initially uncertain whether executory interests were destructible or indestructible. In a case decided in 1620, **Pells v. Brown**, Cro. Jac. 490, 79 Eng. Rep. 504 (1620), however, the common law judges finally decided that executory interests were indestructible.

> *We offer the dates of these old cases somewhat hesitantly. Consider the following exchange between the Court and the Reporter in* **Purefoy v. Rogers**, *2 Wm. Saund. 380, 381, 85 Eng. Rep. 1181, 1182 (1670).*
>
> **In the Court's opinion**: *"... their first son, who was born on the 8th January 1649*...."*
>
> **The Court's footnote**: *"*This date is evidently wrong, for it appears ... that the conveyance was made to R.B. and Isabel* **before** *the son was born; and indeed that fact is necessary to the argument (a)."*
>
> **The Reporter's footnote**: *"(a) [However, the date does not appear to be wrong. For according to the old style, the 21st of October 1649, was before the 8th of January 1649, (i.e., 1649-50).]"*

As a result of the decision in *Pells v. Brown*, classification as a contingent remainder rather than an executory interest had important consequences. Contingent remainders would continue to be destructible. Executory interests, on the other hand, would be indestructible. Subsequently, in 1670 in *Purefoy v. Rogers*, the decision was made that a future interest would be construed as a contingent remainder rather than an executory interest if the future interest was capable of taking effect as a contingent remainder. *See* text at Example 12, Chapter Two.

Example 9

O → A for life, remainder to B and his heirs if B reaches 21. (B is 19; A is living.)

B has a contingent remainder because it is possible that B will reach 21 before A dies.

Example 10

$O \rightarrow$ *A for life, and one day later to B and his heirs if B reaches 21.* (A is living; B is 19.)

B has an executory interest because, as the grant is written, there is no chance that B can reach 21 and one day can pass, as provided by the grant, until after A dies.

The two rules of *Pells v. Brown* and *Purefoy v. Rogers* added a good deal of flexibility to the common law of property. A grantor could provide either a destructible or an indestructible interest. In a choice between the two, when the grant was susceptible of being interpreted or construed as creating either a contingent remainder or an expectancy interest, the law preferred the destructible interest.

C. The Rule Against Perpetuities

The course of property law, however, was not smooth. In 1682, in a case called *The Duke of Norfolk's Case*, 3 Ch. Cas. 1 (1681), a principle surfaced that acted as a curb on the executory interest. In *The Duke of Norfolk's Case*, the beginning of what we now call the Rule Against Perpetuities was announced. Over the next 150 years that principle, a true child of the common law system or process would elaborate itself into a system of rules and exceptions with its own logic and policy. (It is true that *The Duke of Norfolk's Case* was an equity case, but that does not diminish the charm of the metaphor.) We have chosen the year 1700 as a date as of which the received common law can be described; that year is chosen partly because by that time the Rule Against Perpetuities had been conceived, if not christened.

The *Duke of Norfolk's Case* decided that executory interests, in order to be valid and enforceable as written, had to be *sure* to become possessory within a certain period. The beginning of the period was the time of the grant—the date we've been calling *Tg*. The endpoint of the period was not set at a fixed number of years. Those early judges could have saved many generations of lawyers and law students considerable trouble by saying that all executory interests must become possessory within fifty years of the time of the grant.

The impetus of the Rule Against Perpetuities, you see, was to keep the original grantor, O, from controlling the disposition of the property through the use of this new, flexible and indestructible executory interest for too long a period after the original conveyance. Allowing O fifty years' worth of control might have been just enough; it certainly would have been easier to apply.

Instead, the endpoint of the Rule's period is set according to the lives of the persons who are alive at *Tg*, the so-called "lives in being" or "measuring lives." The rule as it eventually evolved usually is stated as: "No interest is good unless it must vest, if at all, within 21 years following a life or lives in being at the creation of the interest."

You should recognize that the Rule destroys future interests that do not become vested "soon enough." The Rule limits the impact of future interests by restricting their enforceability. The Rule represents a belief that property is best utilized when the living rather than the dead control its disposition.

The Rule requires two things: that an interest "vest" and that it vest "soon enough." The word "vest" is a term of art; it varies in meaning from one interest to another. The phrase "soon enough" represents a formula. The Rule permits interests to be "unvested" for a limited period of time after certain individuals living on the date of the conveyance have died.

All of the present, possessory estates satisfy the Rule because possessory interests are deemed to be "vested," for purposes of the Rule, from the moment of creation. The three kinds of future interests in a grantor—possibilities of reverter, rights of entry, and reversions—also satisfy the Rule Against Perpetuities because they also are considered "vested" from the moment of creation. Future interests in a grantee, however, involve a more subtle analysis.

The primary purpose of this chapter is to introduce you to the apparent original reason for the Rule—to keep the newly recognized, very flexible and otherwise indestructible executory interest manageable. We will restate the Rule as it applies to executory interests:

> *No executory interest is good unless it must become possessory, if at all, within 21 years following a life or lives in being at the creation of the interest.*

The word "vested" in the general statement of the Rule becomes "possessory" here—the only way an executory interest may vest *is* to become possessory. The period of time allowed by the formula is grasped most clearly by examining selected conveyances.

Have a look at an executory interest that violates the Rule Against Perpetuities:

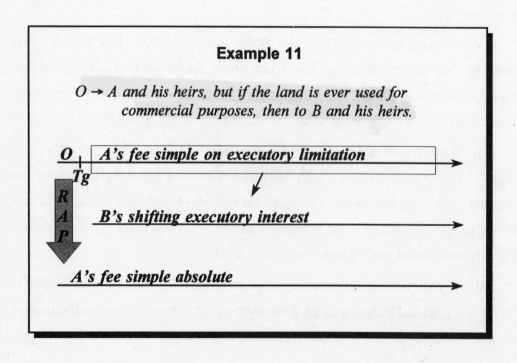

Example 11

O → A and his heirs, but if the land is ever used for commercial purposes, then to B and his heirs.

O A's fee simple on executory limitation
Tg

R
A
P

B's shifting executory interest

A's fee simple absolute

Why? Because B's executory interest will not vest until B's interest becomes possessory; that is, not until if and when the land is used for commercial purposes. There is no guarantee that that event will occur within 21 years of the death of any of the persons alive at the time of the grant. The Rule says "must" and requires just such a guarantee. Hence, B's interest is void. Remove B's interest from the grant and what is left? A fee simple. Simple.

We have used this example several times in the earlier chapters. Note the evolution:

(1) Before 1536 B's interest is void; it's not a remainder.

(2) In 1536, the Statute of Uses allows B's interest; it's a shifting executory interest.

(3) By 1700, the Rule Against Perpetuities has evolved to destroy B's interest as not certain to vest in time.

Here is another example. In this case, the future interest does not offend the Rule.

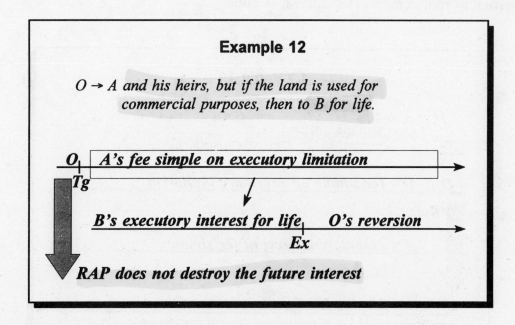

Example 12

$O \rightarrow$ A and his heirs, but if the land is used for commercial purposes, then to B for life.

O
Tg
A's fee simple on executory limitation

B's executory interest for life   O's reversion
Ex

RAP does not destroy the future interest

Why not? Because B's interest will vest, *if ever*, during his life; his interest is in a life estate. That is soon enough for the Rule: B is alive at the time of the grant. B's interest is good.

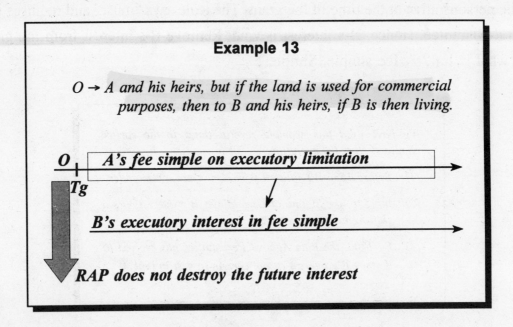

Example 13

O → A and his heirs, but if the land is used for commercial purposes, then to B and his heirs, if B is then living.

A's fee simple on executory limitation

B's executory interest in fee simple

RAP does not destroy the future interest

Once again, B's interest will vest, *if at all*, during B's lifetime, due to the survivorship requirement. B's interest is good.

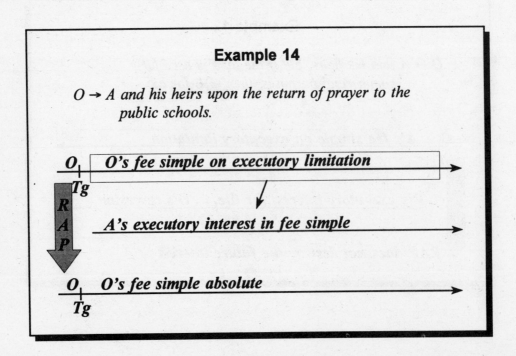

Example 14

O → A and his heirs upon the return of prayer to the public schools.

O's fee simple on executory limitation

A's executory interest in fee simple

O's fee simple absolute

There is no guarantee that the condition will be met within 21 years after the death of the persons alive at *Tg*. A's interest is void.

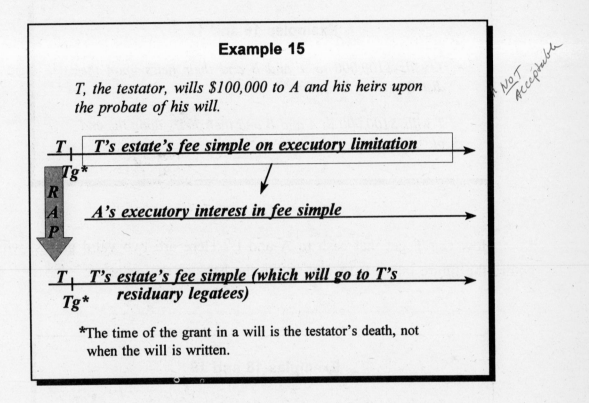

Example 15

T, the testator, wills $100,000 to A and his heirs upon the probate of his will.

T's estate's fee simple on executory limitation

A's executory interest in fee simple

T's estate's fee simple (which will go to T's residuary legatees)

*The time of the grant in a will is the testator's death, not when the will is written.

The result in this grant may be hard to believe. Because the Rule requires the *guarantee* that A's interest will vest within 21 years of the deaths of the persons alive at *Tg*, the future interest created above fails. Justice sometimes works slowly; we can't make that guarantee in this grant, although we recognize the opposite possibility as extremely remote. A's interest is void. This example illustrates the fact that the proper application of the Rule involves some quite fantastic possibilities; in this case, one must envision a very slothful probate court. In other cases, courts have hypothesized children born of very old people, or very young people, or widows who have not yet been born at the time of their husband-to-be's adulthood. All of this shows that when the Rule says "must vest" it means *must* vest.

Here are other examples of future interests that violate the Rule:

Examples 16 and 17

T wills $100,000 to A and B and their heirs upon the distribution of his estate.

T wills $100,000 to A and B and their heirs upon the end of the war.

How can T get that cash to A and B? Here are two valid grants, which require the future interests to vest within the lives of the grantees:

Examples 18 and 19

T wills $100,000 to A and B and their heirs upon the probate of T's will, if either is then living.

T wills $100,000 to A and B for their joint lives and for the life of the survivor, upon the probate of T's will.

Now consider this grant:

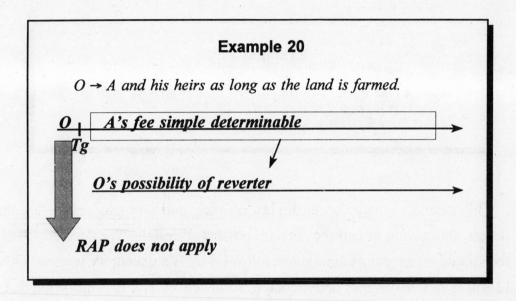

Example 20

$O \rightarrow$ *A and his heirs as long as the land is farmed.*

A's fee simple determinable

O's possibility of reverter

RAP does not apply

"Wait a minute," we can almost hear you say. "Why doesn't the Rule destroy O's possibility of reverter? It won't become possessory until the land is not farmed, which is not certain to be soon enough for the Rule." That is observant, clever and irrelevant. The Rule doesn't apply to possibilities of reverter. Note that, while earlier diagrams said "RAP does not destroy the future interest," here we've said "RAP does not apply." This distinction is pretty fine and mostly historical; recall that the possibility of reverter was in place as a recognized legal future interest well before either the Statute of Uses, the *Duke of Norfolk's Case*, or the Rule against Perpetuities. That future interest, like the right of entry, the reversion and the vested remainder, was deemed "vested" for purposes of the Rule from the moment of creation.

Now this one:

Example 21

*O → A and his heirs as long as the land is farmed, then to
B and his heirs.*

This example was given in the last chapter, and you may recall that there is a debate about what to call the present, possessory estate. We decided to call it A's fee simple on executory limitation, followed by B's executory interest. Others would call it A's fee simple determinable, followed by B's executory interest.

We would all end up at the same place, though, after applying the Rule. We all agree that B's executory interest violates the Rule, for failing to vest in time. Now, those who never changed the name of A's present interest after the Statute of Uses made O's grant valid don't have to do anything now; after the application of the RAP, A has a fee simple determinable and O has a possibility of reverter.

We get the same result by destroying B's future interest, crossing out words until we get to a point where the grant makes sense—that is, back to the word "farmed." What is left is clearly a fee simple determinable, followed, as always, by a possibility of reverter.

So, are you with us? Recall that we renamed A's interest after 1536 so that you could stick with the rule that a possibility of reverter *always* follows a fee simple determinable. Now, when you apply the RAP you have to remember to cross out words only back to the point where the grant makes sense:

Example 22

O → A and his heirs, but if the land is not farmed, then to B and his heirs.

The executory interest is destroyed. Cross out back to "heirs." You can't stop crossing out at "farmed"; if you stop there, what's left doesn't make sense. A has a fee simple and O has nothing.

Note the difference with this example:

Example 23

O → A and his heirs as long as the land is farmed, then to B and his heirs.

The executory interest is destroyed. Cross out back to "farmed." A has a fee simple determinable and O has a possibility of reverter.

The Duke of Norfolk's Case resulted in a curb upon executory interests. The precise workings of the Rule Against Perpetuities were not detailed in this case but rather were worked out in subsequent cases over the next two hundred years. *See generally* J. Dukeminier & S. Johanson, *Family Wealth Transactions: Wills, Trusts and Estates* 970-77 (2d ed. 1978). For example, the traditional formula that describes the period of time allowed by the Rule was not settled until 1833. *Id.* at 976 (citing *Cadell v. Palmer*, 1 Cl. & Fin. 372, 6 Eng. Rep. 956 (H.L. 1832, 1833)). Further, the application of the Rule to class gifts was not stated clearly until 1817. *Id.* at 1006 (citing *Leake v. Robinson*, 2 Mer. 363, 35 Eng. Rep. 979 (Ch. 1817)). The classic formulation of the Rule is found in a treatise written by an American in 1886 [J. Gray, *Rule Against Perpetuities* (1st ed. 1886)]. *Id.* at 970.

The Rule Against Perpetuities was an important and far-reaching reaction to the Statute of Uses. There were others.

The Statute of Wills was passed in 1540 in response to complaints by landowners that the Statute of Uses had eliminated indirect mechanisms for devising land. *See* T. Plucknett, *A Concise History of the Common Law* 587 (5th ed. 1956). Prior to 1536, landowners had devised land by making special conveyances to uses. The Statute of Wills permitted owners of present, possessory estates in land to devise them at common law; an amendment to the Statute of Wills in 1543 permitted those who held certain future interests to devise them. *See* L. Simes & A. Smith, *The Law of Future Interests* § 1901 (2d ed. 1956).

Finally, despite the Statute of Uses, by 1700 real property lawyers had developed a permanent place for equitable property interests. Certain conveyances were recognized as primarily within the jurisdiction of the court of equity. From such exceptional conveyances "to use" came our modern trust. The system of estates in land and future interests in 1700 continues to include equitable as well as legal interests. *See* A. Casner & W. Leach, *Cases and Text on Property* 359-61 (2d ed. 1969).

For purposes of a basic introduction to the Rule, an understanding of its application to executory interests should suffice. Take a look at the review chart that follows, and then try the problems that follow the chart.

D.   Review Table for the RAP

Present, Possessory Interests

- Possessory interests are *vested* and hence no possessory interest is ever destroyed by the RAP. Note, however, that a possessory interest may be *affected* by the RAP. For instance, if an executory interest is destroyed, the preceding present estate might change from a fee simple on executory limitation to a fee simple absolute.

Future Interests

- All the future interests in the grantor—the reversion, the possibility of reverter and the right of entry—are *vested* and never destroyed by the RAP.

- A contingent remainder is destroyed if it is not sure to vest within the period of the Rule.

- An executory interest is destroyed if it is not sure to become possessory within the period of the Rule.

- A vested remainder cannot be destroyed by the Rule. But ...

  - A vested remainder *subject to open* may be affected by the Rule; it will *not* be affected if the class will close within the period of the Rule.

  - A vested remainder subject to divestment will become *indefeasibly vested* if the divesting condition is not certain to happen within the period of the Rule.

E. Review Problem Set (1700)

Please give the state of the title in each of the following problems:

1. *O → A and his heirs as long as the land is farmed, and then to B and his heirs.* (Assume O, A, and B are living.)

   A has ___fee simple determinable___

   B has ___nothing___

   O has ___reverter___

2. *O → B for life, then to B's eldest son for life, then to C and his heirs as long as the land is farmed, then to X and his heirs.* (Assume O, B, C, and X are living and B has no son.)

   B has ___life estate___

   There is a ___*contingent remainder* life estate___ in favor of B's eldest son.

   C has ___*vested remainder* fee simple determinable___

   X has ___nothing___

   O has ___possibility Reverter___

/

3.　　What about:

> $O \rightarrow B$ for life, then to B's eldest son for life, then to C and his heirs, but if liquor is ever sold on the premises during B's or C's lifetime, then to X and his heirs.

B has _life estate_

There is a _contingent life estate_ in favor of B's eldest son

C has _contingent remainder, subject to divestment, in fee_

X has _alternative contingent remainder in fee_

4.　　$O \rightarrow B$ for life, then to the First Baptist Church, but if and when a male descendant of B changes his name to "O," then to such descendant and his heirs. (Assume O and B are living. All of B's living descendants are named "B." B has three living sons.)

B has _life estate_

The First Baptist Church has _fee simple subject to executory limitation_

There is a _executory interest in fee_ in favor of the male descendant of B who changes his name to O.

O has _reversion_

5.   What about: *O → B for life, then to the First Baptist Church, but if and when B or one of his now-living sons changes his name to "O," then to such person and his heirs.*

B has _life_

The First Baptist Church has _contingent remainder, in fee, subject to divestment_

There is a _executory interest_ in favor of B or one of his now-living sons.

O has _nothing_

Answers to Review Problem Set (1700)

Please give the state of the title in each of the following problems:

1.   *O → A and his heirs as long as the land is farmed, and then to B and his heirs.* (Assume O, A, and B are living.)

   Step One: ***Classify the interests without using the RAP.***

   > A—fee simple on executory limitation
   > B—shifting executory interest in fee
   > O—nothing

   Step Two: ***Apply the RAP.***

   > B's executory interest will not necessarily vest in time and is void.

   Step Three: ***What is the result?***

   > Use the "cross-out rule": starting backwards from the end, cross out until the grant makes sense; *i.e.*, back to the word "farmed."
   >
   > A—fee simple determinable
   > B—nothing
   > O—possibility of reverter

2.   *O → B for life, then to B's eldest son for life, then to C and his heirs as long as the land is farmed, then to X and his heirs.* (Assume O, B, C, and X are living and B has no son.)

   Step One: ***Classify the interests without using the RAP.***

   > B—life estate
   > There is a contingent remainder in a life estate in favor of B's eldest son
   > C—vested remainder in fee simple on executory limitation
   > X—shifting executory interest in fee

Step Two: *Apply the RAP.*

X's interest is void under the RAP. The contingent remainder is valid, because it will vest or be destroyed at B's death.

Step Three: *What is the result?*

B—life estate
There is a contingent remainder in a life estate in favor of B's eldest son
C—vested remainder in fee simple determinable
X—nothing
O—possibility of reverter

3. What about:

O → B for life, then to B's eldest son for life, then to C and his heirs, but if liquor is ever sold on the premises during B's or C's lifetime, then to X and his heirs.

In the modified hypothetical, X's interest is a valid executory interest because it will become possessory, if at all, within the lifetime of B and C. Therefore, the state of the title is:

B—life estate.
There is a contingent remainder in a life estate in B's eldest son.
C—vested remainder in fee simple on executory limitation.
X—executory interest in fee.

You might want to call C's interest a vested remainder, subject to divestment, in fee simple. This would be OK, because the divesting condition can be broken either during B's lifetime, when the remainder is still a remainder, or in C's lifetime, after the remainder has become possessory. You might even want to call C's interest a vested remainder, subject to divestment, in fee simple on executory limitation. That's OK, too, though no court that we know of would require that description.

4.   *O → B for life, then to The First Baptist Church, but if and when a male descendant of B changes his name to "O", then to such descendant and his heirs.* (Assume O and B are living. All of B's living descendants are named "B." B has three living sons.)

Are all interests good under the Rule? Why or why not?

Step One: ***Classify the interests without the RAP.***

B—life estate
First Baptist Church—vested remainder, subject to divestment, in fee
There is a shifting executory interest in fee in favor of the male descendant of B who changes his name to O
O—nothing

Step Two: ***Apply the RAP.***

The executory interest is destroyed by the Rule because there is no limit on how distant a descendant might be. It is certainly possible that a descendant could change names, making the executory interest possessory, more than 21 years after O, B and all three of B's sons are dead.

Step Three: ***What is the result of avoiding B's interest?***

Cross out back to "Church":

B—life estate
Church—vested remainder in fee
Male descendant of B who changes his name to O—nothing
O—nothing

5. What about:

    O → B for life, then to The First Baptist Church, but if and when B or one of his now-living sons changes his name to "O," then to such person and his heirs.

    In the modified hypothetical, the executory interest is valid because it will become possessory, if at all, in the lifetime of B and his three living sons, all of whom are helpful lives in being at Tg. Therefore, the state of the title is: B has a life estate, the Church has a vested remainder, subject to divestment, in fee, and there is an executory interest in favor of such of B or his three sons as comply with the condition. O has nothing.

CHAPTER SIX

A FEW INTERESTING COMPLEXITIES

In this chapter, we present some miscellaneous complexities. The system of estates in land and future interests that you have learned so far was supplemented at common law by conceptual accidents, common law pragmatism, and additional policy choices reflected in interpretive rules, called rules of law or rules of construction. We have selected some of the more famous examples to illustrate graphically.

Our selection of the complexities to be offered here is pretty idiosyncratic and we have made decisions more based on what has caught our interest and what we think makes a good teaching point than what has much relevance for your later practice, or even for your present Property course. We hope you find some, if not all, of what follows interesting, but we doubt that your Property teacher will cover all this material. Nevertheless, we have included the material that follows in the hope that some of it will enable you to practice what you have learned, as well as inspire you to ask questions that you can either answer yourself or ask in class.

A.   The Life Estate Determinable

You have seen a great deal of flexibility in the various interests presented so far. For example, you have seen that a remainder can be vested or contingent, and that a vested remainder can be vested subject to open, vested subject to divestment or indefeasibly vested. The common law may have been quite strict *within* the various categories, but it was creative, at least, in the number of categories that were allowed.

You will see that again as we look at the Life Estate Determinable. Start with a look at the chart on the following page, a chart that you may have begun to formulate in your own mind.

Opportunities for the Grantor to Put
Conditions on the Grantee's Possession

	Without Express Condition	*Determinable*	*On Condition Subsequent*	*On Executory Limitation*
Fee Simple	✓	✓	✓	✓
Fee Tail	✓			
Life Estate	✓	*	This may not have been permitted at common law	This is permissible only if clearly expressed

We have discussed the checked squares. Consider the square marked *:

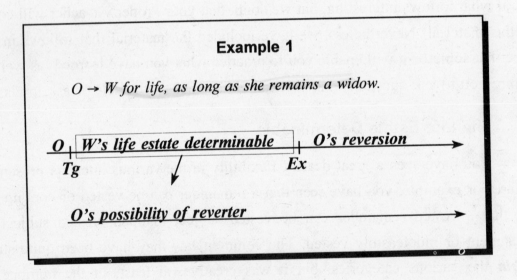

Example 1

O → W for life, as long as she remains a widow.

| O | W's life estate determinable | O's reversion |

O's possibility of reverter

Here, in a life estate determinable, O appears to have retained two future interests: a reversion following W's life estate and a possibility of reverter if she remarries. The reversion is considered the "larger" or more certain estate and might be said to "swallow" the possibility of reverter:

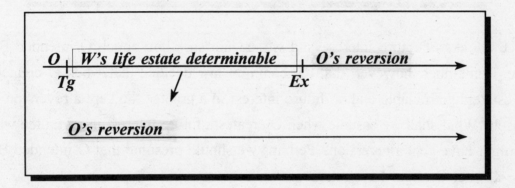

Hence, the term "reversion" refers to two different chunks of future interest:

Hence, the "rule": when O creates a life estate determinable in A and keeps the future interest for himself, he retains a reversion.

Well, then, what about:

Example 2

O → W for life, as long as she remains a widow, then to B and his heirs.

What does B have? O might have intended B to take Blackacre on W's death regardless of whether W remarried, or O might have intended B to take the property only if W remarried. Perhaps O intended B to take in either event. And so on. We have:

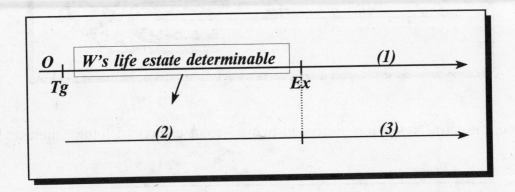

Three chunks of future interest, and we are not sure how much O intended B to have. Remember, however, that the common law decided that when O created a life estate determinable and no future interest in a grantee, he kept a reversion for himself. What shall we assume when O creates a future interest in a grantee when he might have kept a reversion? Perhaps we should presume that O intended B to have all that O might have retained. Presto:

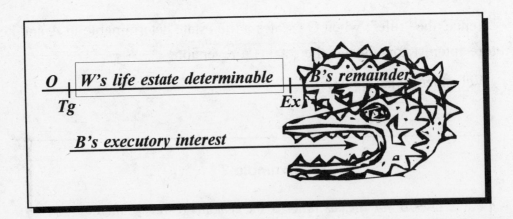

Thus, for our purposes, the future interest in a grantee that follows a life estate determinable is a remainder. This result seems a little anomalous in light of the fact that a remainder could ***not*** follow a ***fee simple*** determinable. Perhaps this is a conceptual accident.

O may, of course, avoid this general rule and create an executory interest in B if he does so clearly. See the note on the chart at the beginning of this chapter under the "Life Estate on Executory Limitation" and the anticipatory note on page 102. Consider the following example:

> ### Example 3
>
> *O → H for life, as long as he remains unmarried, but if H*
> *should remarry, then to B and his heirs.*

Here, it appears that B is to take only in the circumstance that H remarries. We would classify this as follows:

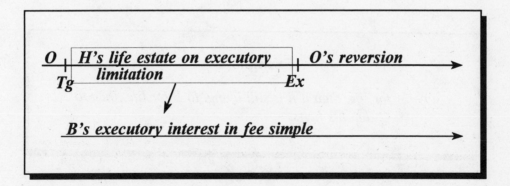

What do you make of this grant?

> ### Example 4
>
> *O → My widow for life, as long as she remains unmarried,*
> *then to my children and their heirs.*

If this grant is in O's will, there is no problem. At O's death his widow is either identifiable or not. If she is, then she takes a life estate determinable and the children have a shared vested remainder in fee simple. If O is not survived by a widow, then that gift fails and the land goes immediately to the children in a shared fee simple absolute. (More on shared present estates later in this chapter.)

But suppose the grant is made while O is still alive. In that case, O's widow is an unknown person. His present wife *might* become his widow, but there is no guarantee of that; she must survive him while still married to be a "widow." Thus, O has retained the present estate, which would be a fee simple on executory limitation. The as-yet unidentifiable widow has an executory interest in a life estate determinable. (No Rule Against Perpetuities problems; do you see why?) We guess that a court would still call the children's interest a remainder, but now it would be a vested remainder subject to open, assuming that one child has already been born, because O is still alive and can have more.

B.   Some Complex Conveyances

Example 5

O → A for life, then if B is still living, to B for life, then to C and his heirs.

What is B's interest? Perhaps you would say B has a contingent remainder in a life estate because of the condition precedent. Look again. The phrase "if B is still living" is surplusage. Of course B has to be living at A's death, or B's life estate cannot take effect. Therefore, you should ignore the surplus words and recognize that B has a vested remainder in a life estate. She may never take possession, because she may predecease A; but the remainder is vested, because there is no stated, meaningful condition precedent. In this case, the common law exercised a thoughtful pragmatism.

Compare:

Example 6

O → A for life, then if B is still living, to B and his heirs.

Here the "if" clause is not surplusage, since without it B would not have to survive A; remember, remainders are inheritable. Thus, the condition stays and B has a contingent remainder in fee simple. O has a reversion.

Example 7

O → A for life and, after A's death, to B and his heirs.

How do you interpret the words "after A's death"? Are they surplusage, since we know that a remainder is to take effect on A's death? Or are they a meaningful condition, implying that B must survive A in order to take the remainder? In the first case, the surplusage would be ignored and B's remainder is vested. In the latter, the remainder is contingent on A's predeceasing B. The issue having been spotted and stated, most of your work is done. The next step is to determine the state of the law in the relevant jurisdiction. The jurisdictions are split on the question. ***See*** L. Simes & A. Smith, ***The Law of Future Interests*** § 585 & cases cited at nn.69, 70 (2d ed. 1956).

Example 8

O → A for life, then to the heirs of B and their heirs, but if at A's death B is still living, then to D and his heirs.

If you too quickly apply the rules you have learned, you may have decided that D has an executory interest in fee simple. Look again. A has a life estate, of course; the next interest is a contingent remainder in the heirs of B, assuming that B is living. Why contingent? Because B's heirs are unidentifiable and will be until B's death. Note, then, that the "but if" clause on D's interest is the condition opposite to that which makes the first remainder contingent. Therefore, D's and B's heirs have alternative contingent remainders. O has a reversion.

Example 9

O → O for life, then to O's three children and their heirs if any of them are then living, but if any of O's children are then dead, then the children of that deceased child shall receive the share of his or her parent, but if any of O's children are then dead without leaving any surviving children, then O's deceased child's share shall go to O's other children.

This grant is essentially that involved in *Spiegel's Estate v. United States*, 335 U.S. 701 (1949). If you analyze it carefully, you will see that O has left himself a very limited reversion: he will take the property only if he outlives all of his children and grandchildren. The property transferred by O was worth about

$1,000,000; based on his life expectancy, O's reversion was worth less than $70. The tax laws in effect at that time required that the entire $1,000,000 be included in O's estate on his death, due to the probably inadvertent retention of the reversion. The conveyance might have been construed otherwise if certain rules of construction were applied liberally. Read on to find out about some of the most famous construction rules at common law.

C. Some Rules of Law and Some Rules of Construction

Previously you were exposed to *Pells v. Brown* and to *Purefoy v. Rogers*. The former is a rule of law; it states an attribute of all executory interests: they are indestructible. The grantor's intent was not relevant. The latter rule is considered a rule of construction; if the grantor had created an interest that was capable of taking effect as a remainder, that interest would be construed as a remainder. The consequence of *Purefoy v. Rogers* was that interests capable of being remainders came under the destructibility doctrine. The destructibility doctrine was a rule of law. It applied independently of the grantor's intent. What follows is an introduction to some of the most familiar rules of law and rules of construction that were received as part of the American common law.

1. The Rule in *Shelley's Case*

The citation to *Shelley's Case* is 1 Co. Rep. 93b, 76 Eng. Rep. 206 (1581). However, the origins of the Rule are said to predate *Shelley's Case* by a good deal. *See* 2A R. Powell, *The Law of Real Property* § 378 (P. Rohan, rev. ed. 1968). This was a rule of law and had nothing to do with the grantor's intent. The Rule in its most classic form provided: If an instrument creates a life estate in A and purports to create a remainder in the heirs of A, the future interest becomes a remainder in fee simple in A.

> *Coke stated the Rule in the following terms: see if you can make sense out of it: "[W]hen the ancestor by any gift or conveyance takes an estate of freehold and in the same gift or conveyance an estate is limited either mediately or immediately to his heirs in fee or in fee tail; that always in such cases 'the heirs' are words of limitation of the estate, and not words of purchase." 1 Coke's Reports 104a, 76 Eng. Rep. 234 (1581) (footnotes omitted).*
>
> **HINT:** *All the present interests of which we have spoken are freeholds. Your introduction to non-freeholds will come when you study landlord-tenant law.*

Consider the following:

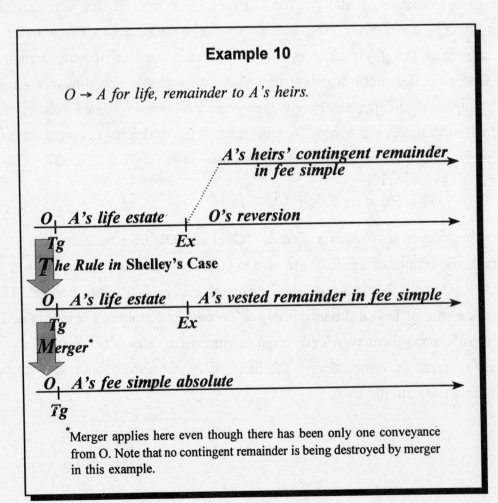

Example 10

O → A for life, remainder to A's heirs.

*A's heirs' contingent remainder
in fee simple*

O | *A's life estate*   *O's reversion*
Tg   Ex

The Rule in Shelley's Case

O | *A's life estate*   *A's vested remainder in fee simple*
Tg   Ex

*Merger**

O | *A's fee simple absolute*
Tg

*Merger applies here even though there has been only one conveyance from O. Note that no contingent remainder is being destroyed by merger in this example.

Why would this conveyance appeal to O? Why isn't it the same as $O \rightarrow A$ *and his heirs*? Remember that in $O \rightarrow A$ *and his heirs*, A may sell all of Blackacre, leaving his heirs-to-be with nothing. In $O \rightarrow A$ *for life, then to A's heirs*, save for the Rule in **Shelley's Case**, A may sell only his life estate. *See* Example 25 in Chapter Two.

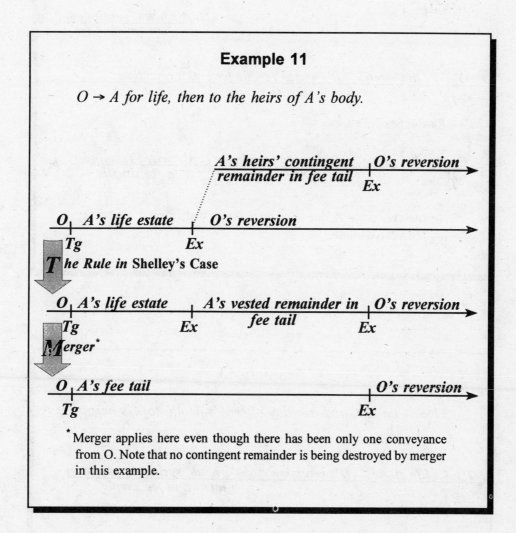

Example 11

$O \rightarrow A$ *for life, then to the heirs of A's body.*

* Merger applies here even though there has been only one conveyance from O. Note that no contingent remainder is being destroyed by merger in this example.

Example 12

O → A for life, then to B for life, remainder to A's heirs.

*A's heirs' contingent
remainder in fee
simple*

O | *A's life estate* | *B's vested remainder
for life* | *O's reversion*
Tg | | *Ex* | *Ex*

***T**he Rule in* Shelley's Case

O | *A's life estate* | *B's vested remainder
for life* | *A's vested remainder
in fee simple*
Tg | | *Ex* | *Ex*

No merger, since A does not own the vested interest next after
his possessive estate.

Example 13

O → A for life, and one day after A's death, to A's heirs.

O | *A's life estate* | *O's reversion* | *A's heirs' springing executory
interest in fee simple*
Tg | | *Ex* | *+1*

The Rule in *Shelley's Case* does not apply, since the Rule applies
only to remainders, not to executory interests.

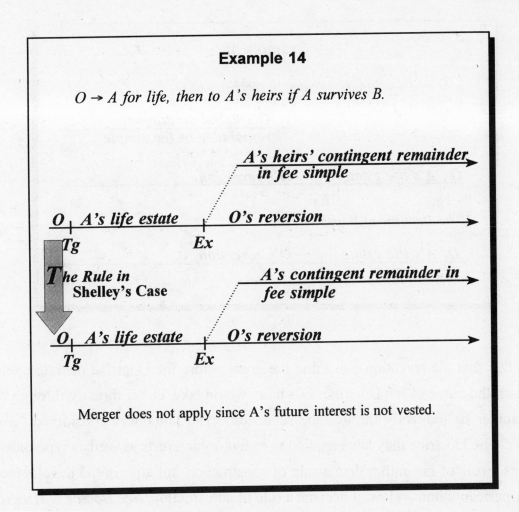

Example 14

O → A for life, then to A's heirs if A survives B.

A's heirs' contingent remainder in fee simple

O   A's life estate   *O's reversion*

Tg   *Ex*

The Rule in Shelley's Case

A's contingent remainder in fee simple

O   A's life estate   *O's reversion*

Tg   *Ex*

Merger does not apply since A's future interest is not vested.

2.   The Doctrine of Worthier Title

The Doctrine of Worthier Title, like the Rule in *Shelley's Case*, is invoked by a grant of a future interest to the heirs of someone. This doctrine applies to the grant of a remainder to the heirs of the grantor. Compare this to the Rule in *Shelley's Case*, which applies to a grant of a remainder to the heirs of the life tenant. The Doctrine of Worthier Title converts the future interest into an interest in the grantor and can be illustrated by the following example:

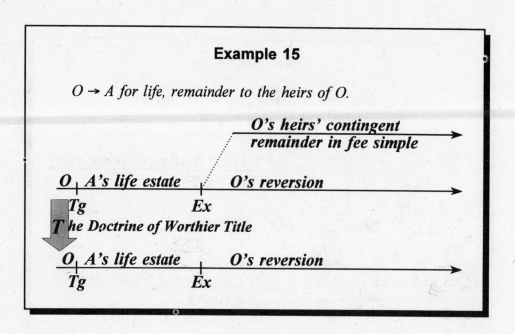

Example 15

O → A for life, remainder to the heirs of O.

O's heirs' contingent
remainder in fee simple

O ⌐ A's life estate   O's reversion
Tg   Ex

The Doctrine of Worthier Title

O ⌐ A's life estate   O's reversion
Tg   Ex

The fact that the reversion existed in the grant before the Doctrine operated helps explain the name of the Doctrine: O's heirs would take, either directly through the remainder or indirectly through the reversion. The latter was considered "worthier." The Doctrine may have applied to executory interests as well as remainders. It was a rule of law rather than a rule of construction initially; in the development of American common law, it became a rule of construction. ***See Doctor v. Hughes***, 225 N.Y. 305, 122 N.E. 221 (1919), for the leading decision. Remember what this difference means: under American common law, strong enough evidence of the grantor's intent to the contrary would overcome the Doctrine. Not so under English common law.

3.   The Rules in *Clobberie's Case*

Clobberie's Case, 2 Vent. 342, 86 Eng. Rep. 476 (1677), had to do with a conveyance of the following form:

> **Example 16**
>
> *O → A and her heirs at 21 or when she marries,*
> *the income to be paid to A until then.*

A died, unmarried, younger than 21, and the question was whether A's heirs took anything. The answer depends, you should recognize, upon whether the grant requires A to survive to the age of 21. If not, then the gift vests at the time of the conveyance and is inherited by her heirs. The court held that the conveyance did not require survival.

The case is remembered for three rules:

(1)   (*The holding*). The grant involved in the case does not require survival by A to the age specified.

(2)   (*In dicta*). "*O → A and her heirs at 21*" requires that A reach 21 in order to take any interest.

(3)   (*In dicta*). "*O → A and her heirs to be paid at 21.*" A's interest vests and will pass to her heirs, even if she dies younger than 21.

These rules are representative of rules that "spell out" implied conditions of survivorship. They are included here so that you will have some exposure to expressions in which the grantor has been found to have intended to require survival. These rules probably are best thought of as rules of construction.

4.   The Rule in *Edwards v. Hammond*

The rule in *Edwards v. Hammond*, 3 Lev. 132, 83 Eng. Rep. 614 (1684), deals with grants in the form of alternative contingent remainders, where:

(a)   the condition precedent to the first remainder follows, grammatically, the words of purchase, and

(b)   the only condition precedent to the first remainder is survival to a certain age.

Before describing what the Rule does to such a grant, let's look at the type of grant that invokes the Rule:

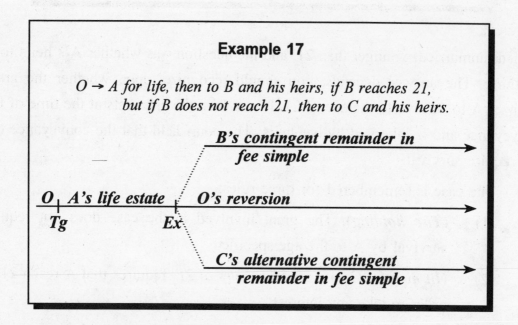

Example 17

O → A for life, then to B and his heirs, if B reaches 21, but if B does not reach 21, then to C and his heirs.

B's contingent remainder in fee simple

O | *A's life estate* | *O's reversion*
Tg | *Ex*

C's alternative contingent remainder in fee simple

The Rule in ***Edwards v. Hammond*** says that the condition precedent to the first remainder is surplusage, and that the first remainder is a vested remainder. As a result, the second "remainder" must be an executory interest. There is no reversion. Presto:

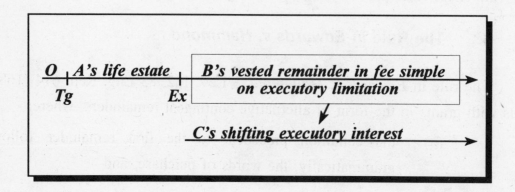

O | *A's life estate* | *B's vested remainder in fee simple on executory limitation*
Tg | *Ex*

C's shifting executory interest

Who cares? Well, note that there are no longer any contingent remainders to be destroyed. In addition, in the days when contingent remainders were inalienable, the grant as originally written restricted the property's alienability much more than the grant as construed under the Rule in *Edwards v. Hammond*. Finally, the result in *Spiegel's Estate v. United States* would change if the Rule were applied.

The Rule in *Edwards v. Hammond* is a rule of construction rather than a rule of law. It represents a constructional preference in favor of a vested remainder over a contingent remainder.

5.   The Rule in *Wild's Case*

Under the Rule in *Wild's Case*, 6 Co. Rep. 16b, 77 Eng. Rep. 277 (1599), the grant *O → A and his children*, **when found in O's will**, should be construed as follows:

(a)   If A has no children on O's death [*O's death is important because the grant must be found in O's will; gifts in a will take effect at the testator's death, not when the will is written*] then A gets a fee tail; *i.e.*, the words "and his children" are read "and the heirs of his body" and are words of limitation.

b)   If A has children on O's death, then A and the children take equal shares; *i.e.*, "and his children" are words of purchase.

The Rule in *Wild's Case* was a rule of construction. The first part (a) seems evidence that a fee tail was a common estate planning choice. The second part (b) makes A and his children concurrent owners of the property. This is your first introduction to grants of the form:

Example 18

O → A and B and their heirs.

---

that is, grants in which possession of Blackacre is shared (or, if you like, Blackacre is "split endwise") and two or more people own simultaneous interests in the land.

> *You've seen concurrent interests before in this book: class gifts and vested remainders, subject to open, are examples. Also, under the Canons of Descent, several sisters inherited concurrently if they had no brothers.*

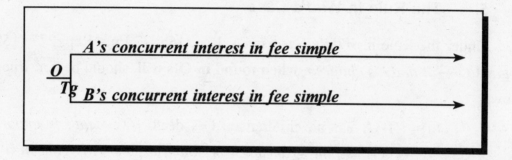

6. Concurrent Ownership

There are three principal ways in which A and B may own Blackacre concurrently:

    (a)   ***Tenancy in Common.***

        A and B each own an undivided half interest in Blackacre. That is specifically not to say that A owns half of Blackacre and B owns the other half. Short of consensual or judicial partition of the estate, neither can point to certain acreage he owns outright. Each owns every square foot of Blackacre in common with the other. The interest of each is alienable and inheritable. If A transfers his interest to C, then B and C are tenants in common.

(b)　　*Joint Tenancy.*

Joint tenants have a right of survivorship. A and B each own an undivided half interest in Blackacre. Should either die, the survivor takes the decedent's share automatically by operation of law. The property does not pass to the decedent's heir and is unaffected by his will. At the early common law, this was the preferred concurrent estate; that is to say, a joint tenancy would be presumed unless the wording of the grant indicated otherwise. What happens if A, say, transferred his interest in Blackacre to C? Then the joint tenancy is severed and B and C became tenants in common. It is inherent in the existence of a joint tenancy that either party may sever it, thereby destroying the other party's right of survivorship. The right of survivorship is a tenuous one.

(c)　　*Marital Estates.*

The law has long supposed that the property of married persons needs a special status for the benefit of the surviving (or lately, the divorcing) spouse. There are two such schemes at present in the United States. The common law's creation was the "estate" known as Tenancy by the Entireties. This was similar to the Joint Tenancy, with its right of survivorship, except that it could not be severed voluntarily by the parties; it took a divorce to end this estate. The civil law's creation was the concept of Community Property, as a result of which the property did not actually "belong" to either husband or wife, but to the "community" represented by their union. Once again, it took a divorce to end the "community." Community property systems are in place in states like Louisiana and California, which trace their laws to France or Spain, and in states like Oregon, which trace their laws to California. The perceived sensibility of the community property system has also influenced the marital property laws of the common law states, so that there is less difference between the systems than there once was.

Much more might be said about concurrent ownership of property; much more undoubtedly will be said in your property course. There are other forms of concurrent ownership that might be discussed, but will not be, in this introductory presentation. You should only be aware that the multiple simultaneous ownership of Blackacre is not unusual.

The foregoing complexities should serve to remind you that the system we have presented to this point is much simplified. We feel that this presentation provides a solid base on which to build later understanding, but do not lose sight of the fact that we are engaging in an oversimplification of the law of estates in land and future interests. The cases, treatises and courses in real property will continue the explanation begun here and enrich your understanding.

Look over the chart on the next page and try your hand at the review problems that follow it:

D. Review Chart

THE ESTATES
• **PRESENT ESTATES**
• Fee Simple
• Fee Tail

• Life Estate
    Life Estate *Pur Autre Vie*
    Life Estate Determinable

• Fee Simple Determinable
• Fee Simple on Condition Subsequent
• Fee Simple on Executory Limitation
• **FUTURE INTERESTS**

• Reversion
    Following an expirable estate
    Following a contingent remainder
    Following alternative contingent remainders
    Preceding some executory interests
    Following a life estate determinable

• Possibility of Reverter
• Right of Entry

• Remainders
    Indefeasibly vested
    Vested, subject to divestment
    Vested, subject to open
    Contingent
    Alternative contingent

• Executory Interests
RULES OF CONSTRUCTION AND RULES OF LAW
• The Rule Against Perpetuities
• The Rule in *Shelley's Case*
• Doctrine of Worthier Title
• The Rules in *Clobberie's Case*
• The Rule in *Edwards v. Hammond*
• The Rule in *Wild's Case*
• Concurrent Interests

E. Review Problem Set

Please give the state of the title in each of the following as it would be at the common law in 1700. Assume that O has a fee simple absolute prior to the conveyance. You must give the state of the title for each of the separate fact situations. All fact patterns are to be treated cumulatively.

1. *O → A for life, as long as she practices law.*

    (a) A is alive and practicing law.

    (b) A is disbarred and forbidden to practice law ever again.

2. *O → A for life, then to A's children and their heirs.*

    (a) A is living and has 2 children, B and C.

    (b) A dies.

3. *O → A for life, then to the heirs of O.* (Assume A and O are living.)

4. *O → A for life, then one year after A's death to the heirs of O.*

5. *O → A for life, then to B for life, then to A's heirs.*

    (a) A and B are living.

    (b)   A dies, intestate, leaving as his only heir, X.

    (c)   B dies.

6.   *O → A and his heirs thirty years from the date of A's birth.*

    (a)   O is living. A is 10 years old.

    (b)   A dies on his 29th birthday leaving as his only heir B.

    (c)   One year passes.

7.   *O → A for life, then to the first son of B who reaches 21 and his heirs, but if no son of B reaches 21, to A's heirs.*

    (a)   A and B are alive. C, B's only son, is 19.

    (b)   O conveys his interest to C.

    (c)   C dies at 20, leaving E as his heir.

    (d)   B dies.

8. *O → A for life, then to the first child of A to graduate from law school and his or her heirs.*

   (a)   A is living. A has two children, S and D, who are both enrolled in law school.

   (b)   D drops out of law school and enrolls in med school.

   (c)   O conveys his reversion to A.

9. *O → A for life, then to the children of B who survive B and their heirs.*

   (a)   A and B are alive. B has no children.

   (b)   B has a child, X.

   (c)   A renounces the life estate.

10. *O → A for the life of O, then to B for life if B survives O.*

   (a)   A and B are living.

   (b)   O dies, leaving a will in favor of X.

11.   *O → A for life, then to B for life, then if C survives A and B, to C and his heirs.*

  (a)   A, B and C are living.

  (b)   O conveys his reversion to A.

  (c)   B dies.

12.   *O → O for the life of W, then to S and his heirs if S reaches 21, but if S does not reach 21, then to D and her heirs.*

  (a)   W, S and D are alive.

  (b)   W dies. S is 19.

  (c)   S celebrates his 21st birthday.

13.   *O → D and her children by A. (The conveyance is by will.)*

  (a)   D and A are alive. D and A have no children.

  (b)   D and A have a son.

Answers to Review Problem Set

Please give the state of the title in each of the following as it would be at the common law in 1700. Assume that O has a fee simple absolute prior to the conveyance. You must give the state of the title for each of the separate fact situations. All fact patterns are to be treated cumulatively.

1.   *O → A for life, as long as she practices law.*

     (a)   A is alive and practicing law.

         A has a life estate determinable.
         O has a reversion.

     (b)   A is disbarred and forbidden to practice law ever again.

         O has a fee simple absolute.

2.   *O → A for life, then to A's children and their heirs.*

     (a)   A is living and has 2 children, B and C.

         A has a life estate.
         B and C have a vested remainder, subject to open, in fee simple.

> *The Rule in* **Shelley's Case** *does not apply in this situation because the conveyance does not create a remainder in the heirs of A. The conveyance creates a remainder in A's children. While A's children are often the heirs of A, they are not the only possible heirs of A. If B and C were to predecease A, without wills, they would not be her heirs and their heirs would inherit the vested remainder.*

     (b)   A dies.

         B and C have a fee simple, as joint tenants.

3. *O → A for life, then to the heirs of O.* (Assume A and O are living.)

   A has a life estate.
   O has a reversion, due to the Doctrine of Worthier Title.

4. *O → A for life, then one year after A's death to the heirs of O.*

   A has a life estate.
   O has a reversion and an executory interest.

> *Before applying the Doctrine of Worthier Title, the state of the title is: A has a life estate; the heirs of O have a springing executory interest; and O has a reversion. We have applied the Doctrine because it may have applied to executory interests. We have not applied the doctrine of merger, because we are not sure an executory interest should be considered "vested" for purposes of merger.*

5. *O → A for life, then to B for life, then to A's heirs.*

   (a) A and B are living.

      A has a life estate and a vested remainder in fee simple. (Merger does not occur here because A's interests are separated by a vested remainder.)
      B has a vested remainder in a life estate.

   (b) A dies, intestate, leaving as his only heir, X.

      B has a life estate.
      X has a vested remainder in fee simple.

   (c) B dies.

      X has a fee simple.

6. *O → A and his heirs thirty years from the date of A's birth.*

   (a) O is living. A is 10 years old.

      O has a fee simple on executory limitation.
      A has a springing executory interest in fee simple.

    (b)   A dies on his 29th birthday leaving as his only heir B.

          No change except B has A's executory interest.

    (c)   One year passes.

          B has a fee simple.

7.   *O → A for life, then to the first son of B who reaches 21 and his heirs, but if no son of B reaches 21, to A's heirs.*

    (a)   A and B are alive. C, B's only son, is 19.

          A has a life estate. There is a contingent remainder in fee simple in favor of the first son of B who reaches 21. (***Edwards v. Hammond*** does not apply because in this example the common law judges thought the age contingency was not surplus, but was in fact an essential part of the description of the remainderman.)

          A has an alternative contingent remainder in fee simple, due to the Rule in ***Shelley's Case.***

          O has a reversion.

    (b)   O conveys his interest to C.

          No change except C has O's reversion.

    (c)   C dies at 20, leaving E as his heir.

          No change except that E has the reversion that was C's. The contingent remainder is not destroyed because it is still possible that B will have a son who will reach 21 before A dies.

    (d)   B dies.

          A has a fee simple absolute. The first contingent remainder is destroyed, A's alternative contingent remainder vests, destroying the reversion. A's life estate and vested remainder merge into a fee simple.

8.   *O → A for life, then to the first child of A to graduate from law school and his or her heirs.*

    (a)   A is living. A has two children, S and D, who are both enrolled in law school.

          A has a life estate.

          First child who graduates has a contingent remainder in fee simple.

          O has a reversion.

    (b)   D drops out of school and enrolls in med school.

        No change.

    (c)   O conveys his reversion to A.

        A has a fee simple absolute, due to merger.

9.   *O → A for life, then to the children of B who survive B and their heirs.*

    (a)   A and B are alive. B has no children.

        A has a life estate.
        There is a contingent remainder in fee simple in favor of the children of B who survive B.
        O has a reversion.

    (b)   B has a child, X.

        No change.

    (c)   A renounces the life estate.

        O has a fee simple absolute, because the contingent remainders are destroyed and the reversion becomes possessory.

10.   *O → A for the life of O, then to B for life if B survives O.*

    (a)   A and B are living.

        A has a life estate *pur autre vie*.
        B has a vested remainder in a life estate, because the condition on the life estate is surplusage
        O has a reversion.

    (b)   O dies, leaving a will in favor of X.

        B has a life estate.

        X has a reversion.

11.   *O → A for life, then to B for life, then if C survives A and B, to C and his heirs.*

    (a)   A, B and C are living.

        A has a life estate.

B has a vested remainder in a life estate.
C has a contingent remainder in fee simple.
O has a reversion.

(b) O conveys his reversion to A.

A has a life estate and a reversion.
B has a vested remainder in a life estate.
C has a contingent remainder in fee simple.

(c) B dies.

A has a fee simple. A's life estate and reversion are no longer separated
  by a vested remainder, so they merge.

12. *O → O for the life of W, then to S and his heirs, if S reaches 21, but
  if S does not reach 21, then to D and her heirs.*

(a) W, S and D are alive.

O has a life estate *pur autre vie*.
S has a vested remainder, subject to divestment, in fee, as a result of the
  Rule in *Edwards v. Hammond*.
D has a shifting executory interest in fee simple.

(b) W dies. S is 19.

S has a fee simple on executory limitation. D has a shifting executory
  interest in fee simple.

(c) S celebrates his 21st birthday.

S has a fee simple absolute.

13. *O → D and her children by A.* (The conveyance is by will.)

(a) D and A are alive. D and A have no children.

D has a fee tail special.
The beneficiaries of O's will have a reversion.

(b) D and A have a son.

No change.

CHAPTER SEVEN

STATUTORY MODIFICATIONS

A.   Introduction

You now have mastered a simplified system that represents the common law of estates in land and future interests as of 1700. When you are asked in this chapter or the appendices to analyze a grant under the common law, you should apply the basic system you learned in Chapters One through Six. What of the more modern law?

England in 1925 enacted statutes which reformed the system and made much of the above obsolete. Modern simplification of property law in England occurred in the early twentieth century with a series of laws. Much of the reform legislation was enacted in 1925 and went into effect on January 1, 1926. *See* C. Moynihan, *Introduction to the Law of Real Property* 25 (1962). The reform legislation seems to have been both technical and comprehensive. For example, the 1925 legislation includes:

(1)   Law of Property Act of 1925 (15 Geo. V, c. 20),
(2)   Settled Land Act of 1925 (15 Geo. V, c. 18),
(3)   The Trustees Act of 1925 (15 Geo. V, c. 19),
(4)   The Land Charges Act of 1925 (15 Geo. V, c. 22),
(5)   The Administration of Estates Act of 1925 (15 Geo. V, c. 23), and
(6)   Land Registration Act of 1925 (15 Geo. V, c. 21)

The legislation was designed to give effect to the intent of the grantor while at the same time obtaining the greatest freedom of alienability of land for commercial purposes. *See* Meschke, *Estates in North Dakota*, 30 N.D.L. Rev. 289 (1954); *see also* J. Cribbett, *Principles of the Law of Property* 37, 308-09 (2d ed. 1975).

In the United States, however, there has never been such a sweeping reform, and modification of the old common law system has been piecemeal and state by state. In making changes, state legislatures often have used the vocabulary of the common law. Because changes have been piecemeal and have relied on common law terms, you are likely to find that understanding a change made in your jurisdiction requires you to recall or determine the common law result the legislature was trying to change, as well as to use the vocabulary you have acquired in applying a statute. The good news is that there have not been very many such changes, and that similar statutes exist in many states. However, we do want to give you a chance to test your new vocabulary and analytical skills on the most public vestige of the common law of estates in land and future interests: state statutes that codify, modify or wholly reform various aspects of the systems you have learned.

In addition, we want to suggest the kinds of changes you might expect to find in the statutes that govern your jurisdiction. We believe that you will have an easier time reading those statutes if you approach them with a mental checklist of typical statutory changes. Once you have such a checklist, we think you will have a good foundation from which to begin to study the American case law and, in particular, the law of the jurisdiction in which you will practice.

Below we survey typical statutory changes in the common law of estates in land and future interests. The survey includes text, examples, problems and answers. An appendix to this text includes selected statutes from several jurisdictions. We will quote or cite to some of these statutes. We hope that this presentation will help you identify and study the relevant statutes in your state.

B. English Common Law Estates in Land and Future Interests as Modified by American Statutes

In many, if not all, states you will encounter statutes that affect the common law rules governing the creation of the present, possessory estate. For example, in many states you will find a statute similar to CAL. CIV. CODE § 1072 (West 1982), which provides that "[w]ords of inheritance or succession are not requisite to transfer a fee in real property." What does such a statute mean? That's right. If $O \rightarrow A$, the absence of the words "and her heirs" does not preclude the recognition of a fee simple interest in A. N.D. CENT. CODE § 47-09-15 (1978) is similar. You might ask whether there are statutes that clearly say what it is that A does have. And there are, in California and North Dakota as well as elsewhere. CAL. CIV. CODE § 1105 provides that "[a] fee simple title is presumed to be intended to pass by a grant of real property, unless it appears from the grant that a lesser estate was intended." N.D. CENT. CODE § 47-10-13 is virtually identical.

What do you think about the following statutory provision?

> Every estate in lands which shall be granted, conveyed or bequeathed, although other words heretofore necessary to transfer an estate of inheritance is not added, shall be deemed a fee simple estate of inheritance, if a less estate is not limited by express words, or do not appear to have been granted, conveyed or bequeathed by construction or operation of law.

See ILL. ANN. STAT. ch. 30, ¶ 12 (Smith Hurd 1969). This single statute accomplishes two goals. Can you identify both, based on the legislation in California and North Dakota quoted above? That's right. The legislature has provided that the phrase "and her heirs" is unnecessary to the creation of a fee interest. The legislature also has indicated that the central question is what the creator of the conveyance or devise intended to give and provided a presumption that he or she intended to create a fee simple absolute. N.M. STAT. ANN. § 47-1-33 (1978) is similar.

Now, suppose the conveyance is *O → A as long as she remains unmarried*. Does A have a life estate determinable or a fee simple determinable? The answer is, it depends. Under the statutes mentioned above, the presumption would be a fee simple determinable. However, in real life, conveyances and devises are made in documents that contain many words, and there will be other evidence of O's intent at the time he or she made the gift. *See, e.g., Lewis v. Searles*, 452 S.W. 153 (Mo. 1970). As a result, the ultimate answer to the question of what A has as a result of O's gift will depend on how the document is interpreted or construed, and that may turn on what other evidence of O's intent is available and admissible. The bottom line is that the statutory preference for a fee simple and the elimination of the need for words of inheritance gives rise to new construction problems, problems the common law rules seem to avoid.

What good is your vocabulary then, and to what use may you put your facility with the kinds of examples and problems, sometimes referred to as "skeleton grants," this book contains? Well, we think that you now have a basic skill that will help you both in locating and understanding statutes and in reading and analyzing cases and, later, documents. We think that the facility you have acquired with "skeleton grants" gives you the power to reduce the language of statutes, cases, and documents to simpler forms and, having reduced them, to identify the range of possible meanings. Thereafter, we think you will be in a position to search for persuasive or controlling authorities and to argue policy. Whether you are litigating, trying to settle a case, or drafting documents, your facility with "skeleton grants" and the knowledge of the common law that facility expresses should be helpful.

Let's try another example. But first, we should say that in many, if not all, states you will find a statute that modifies the common law fee tail. Suppose you encounter the conveyance, *O → A and the heirs of his body*, in Illinois, which has the following provision:

> In cases where, by the common law, any person or persons might hereafter become the owner of, without applying the rule of property known as the rule in Shelley's Case, in fee tail, of any lands, tenements or hereditaments, by virtue of any legacy, gift, grant or other conveyance, hereafter to be made, or by any other means whatsoever, such person or persons, instead of being or becoming the owner thereof in fee tail, shall be deemed and adjudged to be, and become the owner thereof, for his or her natural life only, and the remainder shall pass in fee simple absolute, to the person or persons to whom the estate tail would, on the death of the first grantee, legatee or donee in tail, first pass according to the course of the common law, by virtue of such legacy, gift, grant or conveyance.

See ILL. ANN. STAT. ch. 30, ¶ 5 (Smith Hurd 1969).

In the conveyance *O → A and the heirs of his body*, at common law A had a fee tail and O had a reversion. What does the statute seem to you to do with those interests? Take your time; think of the "skeleton grant" and see if you can find, first, what the legislature has said A will have. That's right, the statute gives A a life estate. How about A's children? That's right; they have a remainder. What kind of a remainder do they have? The answer is, it depends on whether A has any children. If A has a child or children, he, she or they have a vested remainder, subject to open, in fee simple; if A does not, there is a contingent remainder in fee simple in A's unborn children, and O has a reversion.

There is actually case authority in Illinois for this result. We thought you might like to read it for yourself. ***Doney v. Clipson***, 120 N.E. 571, 571 (Ill. 1918), explains the result:

> A granting clause in a deed substantially in the language 'to A and the heirs of his body' defines the estate granted as a fee tail at common law, which ... our Conveyance Act has turned into a life estate in A with a remainder in fee to his children, contingent until their birth if he has none, but vested if he has a child, subject to open and let in after-born children.

Henry v. Metz, 46 N.E.2d 945, 949 (Ill. 1943), describes the statute set out above as creating a "remainder vested in the children, which opens up to let in after-born children of a life tenant."

Other states have taken a different tack. Suppose you encounter the conveyance *O → A and the heirs of his body* in California, which has the following provision:

> Estates tail are abolished, and every estate which would be at common law adjudged to be a fee tail is a fee simple; and if no valid remainder is limited thereon, is a fee simple absolute.

See CAL. CIV. CODE § 763. What do you think? The statute seems pretty straightforward, doesn't it? A has a fee simple. O has nothing.

Now, suppose you encounter the conveyance *O → A and the heirs of his body, then to B and his heirs*, again in California, which has the following additional provision:

> Where a remainder in fee is limited upon any estate, which would by the common law be adjudged a fee tail, such remainder is valid as a contingent limitation upon a fee, and vests in possession on the death of the first taker, without issue living at the time of his death.

See CAL. CIV. CODE § 764. Now, what do you think? It is a little harder in this example to determine what O has given A. However, the statute refers to a "contingent limitation upon a fee." Further, California has a statute that might be viewed as a constructional preference in favor of a fee. *See* CAL. CIV. CODE § 1105. Based on all of these legislative signals, we think the state of the title in this example would be that A has a fee simple on executory limitation and B has an executory interest in fee.

What happens if A dies, leaving a child? The statute seems to provide for A's losing his interest only if he dies without leaving any surviving issue. If A dies intestate, and the child is his only heir, the result looks very much like the result achieved with a fee tail. A's child acquires title. However, there is a significant difference. A's child, if he or she acquires title, has acquired title to a fee simple, an interest that can be sold or devised or inherited by someone other than a lineal descendant.

In addition to modification of the common law rule governing the creation of a fee simple and statutory substitution of interests for the common law estate of fee tail, there have been other modifications. Let's take two other examples.

Suppose you encounter a conveyance like this: *O → A and her heirs as long as the land is farmed.* Or one like this: *O → A and her heirs, but if the land ceases to be farmed, then O and his heirs may reenter and claim the land.* The good news is that in most states the classification scheme you have learned is alive and well; it is appropriate to characterize A's interest in the first example as a fee simple determinable and in the second as a fee simple on condition subsequent, and it is appropriate to characterize O's interest in the first example as a possibility of reverter and in the second as a right of entry or power of termination.

California, however, has the following statute:

> Every estate that would be at common law a fee simple determinable is deemed to be a fee simple subject to a restriction in the form of a condition subsequent. Every interest that would be at common law a possibility of reverter is deemed to be and is enforceable as a power of termination.

See CAL. CIV. CODE § 885.020. How would you apply this statute to the two examples above? The quoted statute does not purport to change the common law result in the second example. However, in the first example, the statute appears to substitute a new term, "fee simple subject to a restriction in the form of a condition subsequent," for the common law fee simple determinable. Further, the statute substitutes the term "power of termination" for the common law possibility of reverter. For other, related changes, *see* CAL. CIV. CODE §§ 885.010, .030, .040.

Now let's suppose the grant or conveyance that these "skeleton grants" represent was made many years ago, let's say in the 1930s. Suppose further that they concern land located in Minnesota, which has the following statute:

> Except for any right to reenter or to repossess as provided in subdivision 3, all private covenants, conditions, or restrictions created by which the title or use of real property is affected, cease to be valid and operative 30 years after the date of the deed, or other instrument, or the date of the probate of the will, creating them, and may be disregarded.

See MINN. STAT. ANN. § 500.20(2a) (West 1990). What does such a statute mean? It appears to restrict the duration of a condition subsequent, doesn't it? Assuming no relevant exception and that thirty years have passed, the proper characterization of the state of the title would seem to be that A has a fee simple absolute and O has nothing. California has a similar provision. *See* CAL. CIV. CODE § 885.030.

In adopting such statutes legislatures are expressing contemporary views about property. In substituting something different for the common law fee tail and in modifying other common law rules, legislatures seem to be limiting the control an owner may retain over his or her grantees. That is not a new phenomenon.

You have already met one form of limitation at common law, the Rule Against Perpetuities. That rule restricts, as you know, the creation of future interests. A number of states now have adopted a particular statutory modification, the Uniform Statutory Rule Against Perpetuities. *See, e.g.,* CAL. PROB. CODE §§ 21200 to 21231 (West 1991); MINN. STAT. ANN. §§ 501A.01 to -.07 (1990); N.M. STAT. ANN. §§ 45-2-1001 to -1006 (1992 Cum. Supp.); N.D. CENT. CODE §§ 47-02-27.1 to -27.5 (Vol. 9B, 1991 Pocket Supp.). Other states have adopted a different modification, *see*, *e.g.*, ILL. STAT. ANN. ch. 30, ¶¶ 191-195, or have retained the common law rule. We will not attempt to illustrate or describe these statutory modifications in this presentation. However, the statutory appendix includes some excerpts from both the uniform act and another statutory modification. You may find it interesting to look at these excerpts.

Because we believe you are equipped to understand these excerpts, we think you now have a foundation for a study of wills and trusts and estate planning. We will not try to do more with statutory modifications to the Rule Against Perpetuities. It is enough, we think, that you know that they exist and that they need to be taken into account in litigating or drafting.

We will mention another kind of statutory restriction on an owner's power to control his or her property after it has been transferred to another. Suppose a conveyance *O → A and his heirs, but if A marries, then to B and his heirs*. Suppose further a statute that provides as follows:

> Conditions imposing restraints upon marriage, except upon the marriage of a minor, or of the widow of the person by whom the condition is imposed, are void. This does not affect limitations when the intent was not to forbid marriage but only to give the use until marriage.

See N.D. CENT. CODE § 47-02-05. In attempting to apply such a statute to the skeleton grant, you would want to know more about O's relationship to A, A's age, and O's purpose in making the conveyance. Assume that the conveyance expresses an intent to forbid marriage. What would be the state of the title? We think that's right; A would have a fee simple.

You probably will have noticed that in describing statutory modifications for the rule governing present, possessory estates, we also found it necessary to describe at least implicitly and sometimes expressly modifications to the correlative future interests. Thus, for example, we implied that the possible existence of a reversion after a fee tail disappears in those jurisdictions that replace the fee tail with a fee simple or a fee simple on executory limitation. *See*, *e.g.*, CAL. CIV. CODE § 763. We also mentioned statutory modifications to the Rule Against Perpetuities and other statutory expressions of public policy that may directly affect the creation of future interests and indirectly the present, possessory estates on which the future interests depend. The only other statutory modification regarding future interests we want you to be aware of at this point is the fact that those interests that were inalienable at common law, by deed or will, tend to become freely alienable by statute. N.D. CENT. CODE § 47-02-18 is illustrative. It provides that "[f]uture interests pass by succession, will or transfer in the same manner as present interests." N.M. STAT. ANN. § 47-1-4 (1978) is comparable, but it refers to conveyances only. However, a number of states, including several of those represented in the appendix, now have adopted the Uniform Probate Code, and in such states, the definition of the estate that passes by intestate succession or will is broad. *See, e.g.*, N.M. STAT. ANN. §§ 45-1-201(A)(9), (31); 2-101 (1978).

Finally, we want to address one aspect of the common law of future interests that might be characterized not as a rule, but rather as an attribute of an interest. That aspect is the common law doctrine of destructibility, that is, that a contingent remainder, as discussed in Chapter Three, at common law was eliminated if it failed to vest before the termination of the prior estate on which it depended.

Again, let's take an example and consider a statute. Suppose *O → A for life, then to the first son of A who reaches 21 and his heirs*. Suppose O and A are living, A has a son S, age 10, and then A dies, survived by S, who is still age 10. At common law, you will remember, O had a fee simple absolute. S's contingent remainder was "destroyed" when A's life estate ended at a time when S could not satisfy the condition. But suppose now this conveyance takes place, and the facts are the same, in a state that has the following statute:

> No future interest shall fail or be defeated by the determination of any precedent estate or interest prior to the happening of the event or contingency on which the future interest is limited to take effect.

See ILL. ANN. STAT. ch. 30, ¶ 40. The statute provides that "[n]o future interest shall fail...." What does that mean? You might find the following statute clearer:

> No future interest, valid in its creation, is defeated by the determination of the precedent interest before the happening of the contingency on which the future interest is limited to take effect, but should such contingency afterwards

happen, the future interest takes effect in the same manner and to the same extent as if the precedent interest had continued to the same period.

See N.D. CENT. CODE § 47-02-32.

Under both statutes, the legislature appears to have intended to abolish the doctrine of destructibility. If the doctrine has been abolished, in the above example, the state of the title after A's death is: O has a fee simple on executory limitation; S has an executory interest in fee. Suppose S dies before reaching 21? We think that O has a fee simple absolute. Do you see why? We would explain that answer by saying that the two statutes actually modify the doctrine of destructibility rather than completely eliminating it. That is, if an owner imposes an otherwise valid condition, whether in connection with a contingent remainder or an executory interest, the beneficiary must satisfy the condition in order to acquire title. You might be interested to know that in at least one state the doctrine has been rejected by opinion, rather than statute. *See ABO Petroleum Corp. v. Amstutz*, 93 N.M. 332, 606 P.2d 278 (1979).

We turn now to other rules and doctrines you are likely to find modified by statute. They include the Rule in *Shelley's Case* and the Doctrine of Worthier Title.

C. Selected Common Law Rules as Modified by American Statutes

In the course of the reception of the common law in this country, one venerable doctrine was abolished by many state legislatures. That doctrine, the Rule in *Shelley's Case*, was abolished by statute in each of the jurisdictions represented in the statutory appendix. We think you will like the effort of the Illinois legislature best: "The rule of property known as the rule in Shelley's Case is abolished." *See* ILL. ANN. STAT. ch. 30, ¶ 186.

If the Rule in *Shelley's Case* is not uppermost in your mind, this example will help. Suppose *O → B for life, then to the heirs of B*. At common law, the phrase "the heirs of B" was considered to provide words of limitation rather than words of purchase. As a consequence, after O made the conveyance described above, there was a vested remainder in fee in B that merged with his or her life estate to create a fee simple absolute. If the rule has been abolished, what is the state of the title?

It may help you answer that question to examine another legislative effort. Consider the following:

> When a remainder is limited to the heirs, or heirs of the body, of a person to whom a life estate in the same property is given, the persons who, on the termination of the life estate are the successors or heirs of the body of the owner for life, are entitled to take by virtue of the remainder so limited to them and not as mere successors of the owner for life.

See N.D. CENT. CODE § 47-04-20. Under such a statute, a conveyance to "the heirs of B" is now viewed as creating an interest in B's heirs, because the statute treats the phrase "the heirs of B" as words of purchase, which identify a grantee rather than describe the estate granted. (That result might be considered bolstered by the modern constructional preference, expressed by statute, for a fee interest.) Therefore, after the rule has been abolished, the state of the title in the example is this: B has a life estate; there is a contingent remainder in the heirs of B; O has a reversion.

Statutes abolishing the Doctrine of Worthier Title are less common in the jurisdictions represented in the appendix. That may be because, as discussed in Chapter Six, the rule became a principle of construction as American case law developed. However, there are examples of statutory modification. CAL. CIV. CODE § 1073 provides:

> The law of this State does not include (1) the common law rule of worthier title that a grantor cannot convey an interest to his own heirs or (2) a presumption or rule of interpretation that a grantor does not intend, by a grant to his own heirs or next of kin, to transfer an interest to them. The meaning of a grant of a legal or equitable interest to a grantor's own heirs or next of kin, however designated, shall be determined by the general rules applicable to the interpretation of grants. This section shall be applied in all cases in which final judgment has not been entered on its effective date.

Similarly, ILL. ANN. STAT. ch. 30, ¶ 188 provides:

> Where a deed, will or other instrument purports to create any present or future interest in real or personal property in the heirs of the maker of the instrument, the heirs shall take, by purchase and not by descent, the interest that

the instrument purports to create. The doctrine of worthier title and the rule of the common law that a grantor cannot create a limitation in favor of his own heirs are abolished.

The California statute might be said to be a little clearer, because it addresses both the English common law principle and the American common law modification. The Illinois statute changing the result at common law is expressed in terms that reflect a similarity between this rule and the Rule in *Shelley's Case*. The Illinois statute expressly describes "the heirs of O" as taking "by purchase," rather than "by descent." In other words, the Illinois legislature treats the phrase "the heirs of O" as words of purchase, rather than as words of limitation. Notice, however, that both statutes modify the common law view that when *O → B for life, then to the heirs of O*, the phrase "heirs of O" described an interest O had retained, rather than an interest he or she had created. Once the Doctrine of Worthier Title is eliminated, when *O → B for life, then to the heirs of O*, B has a life estate, there is a contingent remainder in fee simple in the heirs of O, and O has a reversion. Although either statutory approach works to modify the common law rule, would the result be the same in all cases to which these statutes might be applied? We'll leave you with that question.

There is one more common law rule that we would like you to review. That is the rule that preferred a joint tenancy, rather than a tenancy in common. Thus, if *O → A and B*, it was presumed that A and B held title jointly, with a right of survivorship. The survivors of A and B took title, by virtue of the deed from O, in his or her sole name. What do you understand to be the meaning of a statute such as N.M. STAT. ANN. § 47-1-15 (1978), which provides:

> All interest in any real estate, either granted or bequeathed to two or more persons other than executors or trustees, shall be held in common, unless it be clearly expressed in said grant or bequest that it shall be held by both parties.

That's right. Under such a statute the common law presumption in favor of a joint tenancy, with right of survivorship, is replaced by a statutory preference for a tenancy in common. However, by expressing his or her intent sufficiently, a grantor may create a joint tenancy, with right of survivorship.

Let's review, now, where we are. What follows is based on an original text prepared by Lynn Cianci Eby, University of New Mexico, Class of 1978, for the 1976-77 academic year. Subsequent revisions and expansions were made by the authors, and Professor W. Garrett Flickinger of the University of New Mexico School of Law graciously reviewed some early drafts and made helpful comments. The section should serve as a review of the common law as well as an overview of modern statutory modifications.

D.   Review Outline

1.   The Present, Possessory Estates at English Common Law (About 1700)

a.   Fee Simple Absolute

Problem:	$O \rightarrow A$ *and his heirs*
Facts:	A is living
Answer:	A—fee simple absolute

b.   Fee Tail

Problem:	$O \rightarrow A$ *and the heirs of her body*
Facts:	A is living
Answer:	A—fee tail O—reversion

c.   Life Estate

Problem:	$O \rightarrow A$ *for life*
Facts:	A is living
Answer:	A—life estate O—reversion

Life Estate *Pur Autre Vie*

Problem:　$O \rightarrow A$ *for the life of B*

Facts:　A and B are living

Answer:　A—life estate *pur autre vie*
　　　　　O—reversion

d.　Fee Simple Determinable

Problem:　$O \rightarrow A$ *and her heirs as long as the land is farmed*

Facts:　A is living; the land is being farmed

Answer:　A—fee simple determinable
　　　　　O—possibility of reverter

e.　Fee Simple on Condition Subsequent

Problem:　$O \rightarrow A$ *and her heirs, but if the land ceases to be farmed, then O and his heirs may reenter and claim the land*

Facts:　O and A are living; the land is being farmed

Answer:　A—fee simple on condition subsequent
　　　　　O—right of entry or power of termination

f.　Fee Simple on Executory Limitation

Problem:　$O \rightarrow A$ *and her heirs, but if B returns from Rome, to B and his heirs*

Facts:　A and B are living; B is still in Rome

Answer:　A—fee simple on executory limitation
　　　　　B—shifting executory interest in fee simple

2.   The Present, Possessory Estates as Modified by American Statutes

In the course of the reception of the English common law in this country and in the course of statutory modification over the succeeding years, most of the present, possessory estates have remained intact. The exceptions lie

a.   in the preference for a life estate at common law in the absence of words of inheritance such as "and his heirs." Most jurisdictions now have a statute which provides a constructional preference in favor of a fee simple.

b.   in some states the fee simple determinable and the fee simple on condition subsequent are affected by limitations on the correlative future interests. *See* 4(c), *infra*.

c.   in the modification of the fee tail by statute. States vary in the way in which the fee tail is treated. Some examples follow.

CAL. CIV. CODE § 763

Problem: *0 → A and the heirs of her body*

Facts: A is living

Answer: A—fee simple
O—nothing

ILL. ANN. STAT. ch. 30, ¶ 5

Problem: *O → A and the heirs of her body*

Facts: A is living

Answer: A—life estate

(1)   Children of A (if born)—vested remainder, subject to open, in fee simple

(2)   Children of A (if not born)—contingent remainder in fee simple. In this case, O has a reversion.

3. Future Interests at English Common Law (About 1700)

a. Reversion

(1) Following an Expirable Estate

Problem: $O \rightarrow A$ *while she lives*

Facts: A is living

Answer: A—life estate
O—reversion

Problem: $O \rightarrow A$ *and the heirs of his body*

Facts: A is living

Answer: A—fee tail
O—reversion

(2) Following a Contingent Remainder

Problem: $O \rightarrow A$ *for life, then to B and his heirs if B survives A*

Facts: A and B are living

Answer: A—life estate
B—contingent remainder in fee simple
O—reversion

(3) Following Alternative Contingent Remainders

Problem: $O \rightarrow A$ *for life, then if B marries C, to B and his heirs, but if B does not marry C, then to C and his heirs*

Facts: A, B and C are living

Answer: A—life estate
B—contingent remainder in fee simple
C—alternative contingent remainder in fee simple
O—reversion

(4) Preceding Springing Executory Interest

Problem: *O → A for life, and one day after A's funeral to B and his heirs*

Facts: O, A, and B are living

Answer: A—life estate
B—executory interest in fee simple
O—reversion (in fee simple on executory limitation)

> *The material in parentheses after O's reversion frequently is omitted.*

b. Possibility of Reverter

Problem: *O → A and his heirs until the wind no longer blows through the trees*

Facts: O and A are living

Answer: A—fee simple determinable
O—possibility of reverter

Problem: *O → A and her heirs while she remains married to H*

Facts: O, A and H are living; A and H have married

Answer: A—fee simple determinable
O—possibility of reverter

c. Right of Entry (Power of Termination)

Problem: *O → A and his heirs, provided that if the land is not farmed, then O or his heirs may enter and reclaim the land*

Facts: O and A are living; the land is being farmed

Answer: A—fee simple on condition subsequent
O—right of entry (power of termination)

Problem: *O → A and her heirs on the condition that if the land is not used for library purposes, then O and his heirs may enter and reclaim the land*

Facts: O and A are living; the land is being used as a library

Answer: A—fee simple on condition subsequent
O—right of entry (power of termination)

d. Remainders

(1) Vested Remainder

Problem: *O → A for life, then to B and his heirs*

Facts: A and B are living

Answer: A—life estate
B—vested remainder in fee simple

B's remainder is vested indefeasibly. It is not susceptible to any diminution or loss.

---

(2) Contingent Remainder

Problem: *O → A for life, then if B reaches 21, to B and her heirs*

Facts: A and B are living; B is 15

Answer: A—life estate
B—contingent remainder in fee simple
O—reversion

Problem: $O \rightarrow A$ *for life, then if B survives A, to B and his heirs*

Facts: A and B are living

Answer: A—life estate
B—contingent remainder in fee simple
O—reversion

Here, the condition of survival must be satisfied before B can take the land, so this is a contingent remainder. A reversion always follows a contingent remainder in fee.

Problem: $O \rightarrow A$ *for life, then to A's youngest child living at the time of A's death and that child's heirs*

Facts: A is living

Answer: A—life estate
Child of A—contingent remainder in fee simple
O—reversion

It is contingent because until A dies, it is impossible to determine who, if anyone, will be his youngest child then living. Suppose A is 92 and has two children, P and Q, and that Q is the younger. Still we cannot be sure that Q will be alive when A dies or that he might not still have a younger sibling, so the remainder is contingent.

Problem: $O \rightarrow A$ *for life, then to whoever is dean of the Law School and her heirs*

Facts: A is living

Answer: A—life estate

There is a contingent remainder in fee simple in that person who is dean when A dies

O—reversion

> *The dean's remainder is contingent because the identity of the dean when A dies is unknown. A reversion always follows a contingent remainder in fee.*

---

(3) Alternative Contingent Remainder

Problem: *O → A for life, then if B has married W, to B and his heirs, but if B has not married W, then to C and his heirs*

Facts: A, B, W and C are living; B has not married

Answer: A—life estate

B—contingent remainder in fee simple

C—alternative contingent remainder in fee simple

O—reversion (this always follows contingent remainders, even alternative contingent remainders)

(4) Vested Remainder Subject to Divestment

Problem: *A → B for life, then to C and her heirs, but if C dies without issue surviving her, then to D and his heirs*

Facts: B, C and D are living

Answer: B—life estate

C—vested remainder, subject to divestment, in fee

D—shifting executory interest in fee simple

(5) Vested Remainder Subject to Open

Problem: *A → B for life, then to the children of B and their heirs*

Facts: B is alive and has two children, C and D

Answer: B—life estate

C & D—vested remainder, subject to open, in fee simple, (this is sometimes also called a vested remainder, subject to partial divestment)

e.   Executory Interests

(1) Shifting Executory Interest

Problem: *O → A and her heirs, but if A changes her name, then to B and his heirs*

Facts: A and B are living; A is known as "A"

Answer: A—fee simple on executory limitation

B—shifting executory interest in fee simple

(2) Springing Executory Interest

Problem: *O → S and his heirs upon S's marriage*

Facts: O and S are living; S has not married

Answer: O—fee simple on executory limitation

S—springing executory interest in fee simple

> *Here, O is keeping present possession of the land until S gets married. S has only a future interest. This "freehold" to commence in the future could not be done before 1536; after 1536 it is accomplished with an executory interest.*

4.   Future Interests as Modified by American Statutes

In the course of the reception of English common law and the subsequent statutory modification, the law of future interests has been modified, generally, as follows:

a.   The inalienable interests, and those that were not devisable, tend to become freely alienable. *See, e.g.*, N.M. STAT. ANN. § 47-1-4; N.D. CENT. CODE § 47-02-18.

b.   The possible existence of a reversion after a fee tail disappears in those jurisdictions in which the fee tail is replaced by a fee simple. For example,

Problem: O → A and the heirs of his body

Facts: A is living

CAL. CIV. CODE § 763:

Answer: A—fee simple

Compare, on the other hand, ILL. ANN. STAT. ch. 30, ¶ 5:

Answer: A—life estate
Children of A (if born)—vested remainder, subject to open, in fee simple
Children of A (if not born)—contingent remainder in fee simple. In this case, O has a reversion.

c.   In some jurisdictions statutes may limit the length of life of a possibility of reverter or a right of entry.

d.   A number of jurisdictions have enacted statutory modifications of the Rule Against Perpetuities.

Problem: $O \rightarrow A$ and his heirs, but if the land is used for a farm, then to B and his heirs

Facts: O, A, and B are living

At English common Law:

Answer: A—fee simple
O—nothing
B—nothing

> The gift to B is an executory interest which will not "vest" for purposes of the RAP until the time comes for B or his successors to take possession. That time may come too remotely; **i.e.,** more than 21 years after O, A and B die. Therefore, B's interest is void under the Rule.

Problem: $O \rightarrow A$ and his heirs but if the land is used for a farm during A's lifetime, then to B for life

Facts: O, A, and B are living

At English common law:

Answer: A—fee simple on executory limitation
B—executory interest in a life estate
O—reversion

> B's interest, being a life estate, will come into possession, if at all, within B's own lifetime. Therefore, B's interest satisfies the RAP.

Problem: $O \rightarrow A$ and his heirs but if the land is used for a farm, then to B and his heirs if B is then living

Facts: O, A, and B are living

At English common law:

Answer: A—fee simple on executory limitation
B—executory interest in fee
O—nothing

> *B's interest will come into possession during his lifetime, or fail, by the gift's own terms. The presence of the express condition of survival saves B's gift for purposes of the RAP.*

By statute, such as, *e.g.*, CAL. CIV. CODE §§ 21200, 21201; ILL. STAT. ANN. ch. 30, ¶ 192, the common law may have been superseded or modified. Although these statutes do not appear to change the basic principles illustrated by these examples, you should consider the combined effect of such statutes as CAL. CIV. CODE §§ 885.010, .030, and CAL. PROB. CODE § 21205.

e.   Some jurisdictions have enacted other, specific restrictions on the control a grantor may exercise upon his or her grantees.

f.   The doctrine of destructibility of contingent remainders has been modified by statute.

   Problem: O → A for life, then to the first son of A who reaches 21 and his heirs

   Facts: (i)   O and A are living; A has a son, S, age 10

              (ii) A dies when S is 16

   At English common law:

   Answer: (i)   A—life estate
First son who reaches 21—contingent remainder in fee simple
O—reversion

        (ii)   O—fee simple absolute

By statute, such as, *e.g.*, CAL. CIV. CODE §§ 741, 742; ILL. ANN. STAT. ch. 30 ¶ 40; MINN. STAT. ANN. § 500.15; N.D. CENT. CODE § 47-02-32:

Answer: (i)   A—life estate
                    First son who reaches 21—contingent remainder in fee simple
                    O—reversion

        (ii)   O—fee simple on executory limitation
                    First son who reaches 21—springing executory interest in fee simple

---

Here, S will take if and when he becomes 21. If S does not reach 21 and A has another son who does, that son will take.

---

5.   Selected Rules of Law and Rules of Construction

a.   The Rule in *Shelley's Case*

Problem: *O → B for life, then to C and her heirs if C survives B, and if she does not survive B, then to the heirs of B*

Facts: B and C are living

At English common law:

Answer: B—life estate
              C—contingent remainder in fee simple
              B—alternative contingent remainder in fee simple
              O—reversion

By statute, such as, *e.g.,* CAL. CIV. CODE § 779; ILL. ANN. STAT. ch. 30, ¶ 186; MINN. STAT. ANN. § 500.14(4); N.M. STAT. ANN. § 47-1-19; N.D. CENT. CODE § 47-04-20:

Answer: B—life estate
C—contingent remainder in fee simple
Heirs of B—alternative contingent remainder in fee simple
O—reversion

b. Doctrine of Worthier Title

Problem: *O → B for life, then to the heirs of O*

Facts: O and B are living

At English common law:

Answer: B—life estate
O—reversion

> *O's heirs may inherit the estate by descent upon O's death intestate.*

By statute, such as, *e.g.,* CAL. CIV. CODE § 1073; ILL. ANN. STAT. ch. 30, ¶ 188:

Answer: B—life estate
Heirs of O—contingent remainder in fee simple
O—reversion

c. The Rule in *Clobberie's Case*

Problem: *O → A and her heirs at A's attaining the age of 21.*

Facts: (1) O and A are living.
(2) A dies, at age 19.

At English common law:

Answer: (1)   O—fee simple on executory limitation
                       A—executory interest in fee

              (2)   O has a fee simple absolute

> *The phrase "when A reaches 21" is treated, under* **Clobberie's Case**, *as imposing an implied requirement of survivorship. When A dies at age 19, A's interest is eliminated. This constructional rule generally has not been changed by statute. It is hard to judge how much deference a modern court would pay to it.*

d.   Doctrine of *Edwards v. Hammond*

Problem: *O → A for life, then to B and his heirs if B reaches 21, and if B fails to reach 21, to C and his heirs*

Facts: O, A and B are living; B is 19

At English common law:

Answer: A—life estate
                B—vested remainder, subject to divestment, in fee
                C—executory interest in fee

> *Generally, this constructional preference has not been changed by statute. It is hard to judge how much attention a modern court would pay to it.*

e. Concurrent Estates

Problem: $O \rightarrow A \ and \ B \ and \ their \ heirs$

Facts: (1)   O, A, and B are living
   (2)   A dies, leaving as his only heir X

At English common law:

Answer: (1)   A and B—fee simple as joint tenants
   (2)   B—fee simple absolute

By statute, such as, *e.g.*, CAL. CIV. CODE § 686.; ILL. ANN. STAT. ch. 76, ¶ 1; MINN. STAT. ANN. § 500.19(2); N.M. STAT. ANN. § 47-1-15; N.D. CENT. CODE § 47-02-08:

Answer: (1)   A and B—fee simple as tenants in common
   (2)   X and B—fee simple as tenants in common

f. Rule in *Wild's Case*

Problem: $O \rightarrow A \ and \ his \ children.$ (The conveyance is made by will.)

Facts: (1)   O is dead. A is living and has no children.
   (2)   O is dead. A is living and has one child, C.

At English common law:

Answer: (1)   A has a fee tail.
   (2)   A and C have a fee simple as joint tenants.

> *(1) illustrates the first resolution in Wild's Case and represents a constructional preference for a fee tail in order to accomplish the testator's intent. (2) illustrates a class gift and the common law constructional preference for a joint tenancy. The Rule in* **Wild's Case** *generally has not been changed by statute. The case results are too diverse to treat here. A common modern result in (1) is that A is recognized as having a life estate and there is a contingent remainder in A's unborn children. O's successors have a reversion. A common modern result in (2) is that A and C are recognized as having a fee simple as tenants in common. Both of these results seem consistent with the statutory modifications you have learned.*

E. A Final Problem and Answer

Problem: O → A and her heirs, but if A dies without issue, then to B and his heirs

Facts: O, A and B are living

At common law, the phrase "die without issue" was interpreted as meaning indefinite failure of issue, with the result that A in this example is understood to have a fee tail. B has a vested remainder in fee simple.

Suppose this conveyance takes place in a jurisdiction that has the following statute:

> Where a future interest is limited by a grant to take effect on the death of any person without heirs, or heirs of his body, or without issue, or in equivalent words, such words must be taken to mean successors, or issue living at the death of the person named as ancestor.

See CAL. CIV. CODE § 1071. What do you think this statute is intended to do? What is the state of the title in the above problem under such statute? If you aren't sure, try reading Minn. Stat. Ann. § 500.14(1), N.M. Stat. Ann. § 47-1-18 and N.D. Cent. Code § 47-09-14, all of which are contained in the statutory appendix.

Answer: A—

              B—

              O—

Answer to Final Problem

Problem: $O \rightarrow A$ *and his heirs, but if A dies without issue, then to B and his heirs.*

CAL. CIV. CODE § 1071:

Answer: A—fee simple on executory limitation
        B—executory interest in fee
        O—nothing

By statute in many states the phrase "dies without issue" is to be interpreted or construed as meaning "definite" failure of issue; that is to say, B in the example is viewed as being given a gift that will take effect only if, at A's death, A is not survived by issue. If A is survived by issue at his or her death, A's estate includes a fee simple absolute. That fee will pass pursuant to A's will or, if A dies without a will, to A's heirs under the laws of intestate succession.

> *In Illinois, the answer probably would be the same in that the existing case law seems to permit the common law construction to be overcome with only slight evidence of contrary intent.* **See** *L. Simes & A. Smith,* **The Law of Future Interests** *§ 527, at 499 & n.47 (2d ed. 1956);* **see also Strain v. Sweeney,** *163 Ill. 603 (1896), in which the Illinois court applied the "definite" failure of issue construction as a matter of following the testator's implied intent.*

There are two additional problem sets in the appendices. The set in Appendix I is intended to be answered at common law. The set in Appendix II is intended to be solved at common law as well as under one of the statutory schemes represented in Appendix III. Answers are included for both sets of problems.

APPENDIX I

A PROBLEM SET WITH ANSWERS

Part I

Give the state of the title in 1530.

1. $O \rightarrow A$ *for life, then if B marries C, to B and his heirs.*

    a. Everyone is alive; B is unmarried.

    A has a life estate, B has a contingent remainder in fee and O has a reversion.

    b. $A \rightarrow X$.

    X has a life estate *pur autre vie*, and the rest is unchanged.

    c. $O \rightarrow X$.

    X has a fee simple through application of the doctrine of merger.

2. Same Grant.

    a. $A \rightarrow X$.

    X has a life estate *pur autre vie*, B has a contingent remainder in fee, and O has a reversion.

    b. B marries C.

    X has a life estate *pur autre vie* and B has a vested remainder in fee simple. O has nothing.

206

3.   *O → A for life, then to A's widow for life.*

A has a life estate, there is a contingent remainder for life in whoever becomes A's widow, and O has a reversion.

4.   *O → A for life, then to A's present wife for life.*

A has a life estate and A's wife has a vested remainder for life, if he has a "present wife," which is a legitimate assumption, given O's words. O has a reversion.

5.   *O → A for life, then to W for life.*

A has a life estate, W has a vested remainder for life and O has a reversion.

6.   *O → A for life, then to A's wife for life.*

A has a life estate. Assuming A is unmarried, which is our exam-taking convention, then there is a contingent remainder for life in "A's wife" and O has a reversion.

The difference between Problem 4 and Problem 6 is really an artificial one based on exam-taking convention. In the real world, the question would be O's intent in both cases and, if A was actually married at the time of the grant in 6, then the wife would have a vested remainder for life. (To see why it matters whether her remainder is vested or contingent, see Problem 1(c) above.) If, in the real world, A was unmarried at the time of the grant in Problem 4, then we, and the court, would be a little confused about what O meant. In that event, we would guess that the court would turn 4 into 6.

---

7.   *O → A for life, then to A's widow for life, then to B and his heirs.*

A has a life estate, there is a contingent remainder for life in the woman who becomes A's widow. B has a vested remainder in fee and O has nothing.

8.   *O → A for life, then to A's children and their heirs.*

   a.   O and A are alive; A has no children.

   A has a life estate, there is a contingent remainder in fee in the as-yet non-existent children and O has a reversion.

   b.   S is born.

   A has a life estate, S has a vested remainder, subject to open, in fee. O has nothing.

   c.   D is born.

   No change, except that D now shares in the vested remainder, subject to open, in fee.

   d.   A dies.

   The class closes naturally. S and D share a fee simple as joint tenants with a right of survivorship.

9.   *O → A for life, then to A's grandchildren and their heirs.*

   a.   O and A are alive; A has no grandchildren.

   A has a life estate, there is a contingent remainder in fee in the grandchildren and O has a reversion.

   b.   GS is born.

   A has a life estate and GS has a vested remainder, subject to open, in fee simple. O has nothing.

   c.   GD is born.

   No change, except that GD now shares the vested remainder, subject to open, in fee.

   d.   A dies.

   Naturally, the class is still open, because more grandchildren could be born. But the "Rule of Convenience" closes the class artificially. GS and GD share a fee simple as joint tenants with a right of survivorship.

10. *O → A for life, then to B's children.*

   Assuming no children, as is the exam-taking convention, unless told otherwise, A has a life estate, there is a contingent remainder in B's eventual children, if any, for their collective lives and O has a reversion. If B has a bunch of kids and then A dies, those kids will take, collectively, a life estate.

11. *O → A for life, then to B's heirs.*

   A has a life estate. Assuming B is alive, which is our exam-taking convention, there is a contingent remainder in B's eventual heirs. The phrase "to B's heirs" is read "to B's heir and his heirs." O has a reversion.

12. *O → A for life, then to A's widow for life, then to A's grandchildren and their heirs.*

   A has a life estate, there is a contingent remainder for life in the "widow" and a contingent remainder in fee in the "grandchildren." Here we're using the exam-taking convention that A is alive and has no children, since we're not told otherwise. O has a reversion.

   Suppose A is married to W. No change as we won't know if W will be the "widow" until A dies.

   Suppose a grandchild GD is born. Now A has a life estate, the contingent remainder is the same and GD has a vested remainder, subject to open in fee. O has nothing.

> *This vested remainder might stay open a long, long time. It will not close naturally until the death of the last of A's children, and because A is still alive we can't even be sure that all of those children—let alone the **grandchildren**—are presently alive. Even with the "Rule of Convenience" the remainder will not close until distribution is required, and that is not until the death of the "widow." The common law was willing to imagine that the woman who will eventually become A's widow might herself not even be born yet.*
>
> *So, you can see that in either case, we can't be **certain** that the remainder will close until after the deaths of persons who may not even be born at the time of the grant. The Rule against Perpetuities will evolve to destroy this very patient remainder. In 1700, then, the state of the title is: A has a life estate, there is a contingent remainder in "A's widow" and O has a reversion. This works to control the "dead hand", because relatively "soon" it will go to O's heirs or assigns who then will control the disposition of the property. They can send it to A's grandchildren if that seems appropriate, but the dead O will have no say in the matter.*

Part II

Give the state of the title in 1550:

1.   *O → A and his heirs, but if the land is ever used for commercial purposes, then O may re-enter and claim the land.*

A has a fee simple on condition subsequent; O has a right of entry.

2.   *O → A and his heirs as long as the land is not used for commercial purposes.*

A has a fee simple determinable; O has a possibility of reverter.

3.   *O → A and his heirs, but if the land is ever used for commercial purposes, then to B and his heirs.*

A has a fee simple on executory limitation; B has a shifting executory interest in fee; O has nothing.

4.   *O → A and his heirs, then to B and his heirs.*

A has a fee simple absolute; B and O have nothing.

5.   *O → A for life, and if B is still solvent one year after A's death, to B and his heirs.*

A has a life estate; B has a springing executory interest in fee; O has a reversion.

6.   *O → A for life, then, if B is still solvent, to B and his heirs.*

A has a life estate; B has a contingent remainder in fee simple; O has a reversion.

7. *O → A for life, then to B and his heirs as long as B remains solvent, but if B becomes insolvent, to C and his heirs.*

A has a life estate; B has a vested remainder, subject to divestment, in fee simple; C has a shifting executory interest in fee simple; O has nothing. It is permissible to call B's interest a vested remainder in fee simple on executory limitation.

8. *O → A for life, then to B and his heirs as long as B and his heirs remain solvent, but if any of them become insolvent, to C and his heirs.*

A has a life estate; B has a vested remainder, subject to divestment, in fee simple; C has a shifting executory interest in fee; O has nothing. It is permissible to call B's interest a vested remainder in fee simple on executory limitation.

9. *O → A for life, then to B and his heirs if B is solvent, but if B is insolvent, to C and his heirs.*

A has a life estate; B has a contingent remainder in fee simple; C has an alternative contingent remainder in fee; O has a reversion.

10. *O → A for life, but if A leaves the church, to the church forever.*

A has a life estate subject to an executory interest; the Church has a shifting executory interest in fee; O has a reversion.

11. *O → A for life, then to B and his heirs, but if B uses the land for commercial purposes, to C and his heirs.*

A has a life estate; B has a vested remainder in fee simple on executory limitation; C has a shifting executory interest in fee; O has nothing.

12. *O → A for life, then to B and his heirs, but if the land is used for commercial purposes, to C and his heirs.*

Except for the application of the Rule against Perpetuities, this grant is the same as the previous one.

13.   *O → A for life, then to B and his heirs, but if A becomes a priest, to the Church forever.*

14.   *O → A for life, then to B and his heirs, but if B becomes a priest, to the Church forever.*

15.   *O → A for life, then to B and his heirs, but if B uses the land for commercial purposes, then to the Church forever.*

The "standard" classification of the state of the title in Problems 13 and 14 is exactly the same: A has a life estate; B has a vested remainder, subject to divestment, in fee simple; the Church has a shifting executory interest in fee; O has nothing.

The "advanced" classification would make B's interest in Problem 13 a vested remainder, subject to divestment, in fee simple, because B's interest can only be lost during A's life, while B's interest is still a non-possessory remainder. In Problem 15 (which, for some reason, is nearly identical to Problem 11), B's interest is a vested remainder in fee simple on executory limitation, because B cannot lose his interest in Blackacre until after he comes into possession of it. B's interest in Problem 14 could be lost either before or after it becomes possessory and could be called, most formally, a vested remainder, subject to divestment, in fee simple on executory limitation, to indicate that it could be lost either while it is a remainder or after it becomes possessory. Most courts don't have the patience for such a long term and would call it a vested remainder, subject to divestment, in fee simple.

What would be the state of the title for the grants in Part II in 1700; *i.e.*, after the Rule Against Perpetuities is in place?

The RAP would destroy the executory interest in Grants 3, 8 and 12.

Look carefully at each of the three grants. Those are the ones where the owner of the executory interest must wait, broadly speaking, a long time for it to come into possession: In Grants 3 and 12, until the land is used for commercial purposes; in Grant 8 until any one of B's descendants goes broke.

*Now, of course, either of those eventualities **might** happen in the next week or the next year after Tg. One of the points of the RAP, however, is that we don't wait and see how the world actually turns out. Rather, the validity of the grant must be tested under the RAP at Tg, and the Rule requires **certainty** that all the interests will vest within the period. No matter what period might have been chosen, it is clear that no such certainty would be present for the conditions in grants 3, 8 and 12. Those conditions might still be around and unmet centuries from now. The Statute of Uses may have accepted such extreme flexibility, but the courts that adopted the RAP were not willing to allow O that much power, to leave the state of the title up in the air for centuries, not knowing in whom the interests would vest.*

So, the RAP would destroy the executory interests in grants 3, 8 and 12. Use the "cross-out rule." In grant 3, A has a fee simple absolute and no one else has anything. In grant 8, A has a life estate; B has a vested remainder in fee simple determinable; and O has a possibility of reverter. In grant 12, A has a life estate and B has a vested remainder in fee simple absolute.

APPENDIX II

ANOTHER PROBLEM SET WITH ANSWERS

Instructions:

In each of the hypotheticals, give the state of the title for each of the fact situations as it would exist in England in 1700, and then give the state of the title based on the statutes for one of the jurisdictions represented in Appendix III. In each case, the grantor had a fee simple absolute. If there is more than one set of fact situations for a hypothetical, treat the fact situations as cumulative.

1. *O → A for life, remainder to B and his heirs if B marries C.*

   (a)   O, A, B and C are living; B has not married.

   (b)   B marries C.

   (c)   O conveys all his interest to A and her heirs.

2. *O → A for life, then if B has reached the age of 21, to B and his heirs.*

   (a)   O, A and B are all alive; B is 16.

   (b)   A dies one year later.

3.   *O → A for life, then to A's heirs if A survives B.*

   (a)   O, A, and B are living.

4.   *O → B for life, and one year after B's death to the heirs of B.*

   (a)   O and B are living.

5.   *O → A for life, remainder to B and her heirs if B marries C, and if B does not marry C, to D and his heirs.*

   (a)   O, A, B, C and D are living; B has not married.

   (b)   B marries C.

   (c)   A renounces her life estate.

6.   *O → H for life, then to C and his heirs so long as liquor is not sold on the premises.*

   (a)   O, H, and C are living.

7.   *O → A for life, then to B and the heirs of his body.*

   (a)   O, A, and B are living.

8. $O \rightarrow A$.

(a)   O and A are living.

9. $O \rightarrow A$ *for life, then to A's children and their heirs.*

(a)   O and A are living. A has no children.

(b)   One child, C, is born to A.

10. $O \rightarrow A$ *for life, then to B's heirs.*

(a)   O, A, and B are living

11. $O \rightarrow A$ *until she dies.*

(a)   O and A are living

12. $O \rightarrow A$ *and the heirs of his body, then to the children of B and their heirs.*

(a)   O, A and B are living; A and B have no children. A is married, and B is married.

(b)   A has a child, C.

(c)   B has a child, D.

(d)   B dies.

(e)   A dies with a will leaving all his property to F and his heirs.

13.   *O → C for life, remainder to B for life, then to the heirs of B.*

(a)   O, B and C are all alive.

14.   *O → B for life, remainder to C for life, then to the heirs of B.*

(a)   O, B and C are all alive.

(b)   C dies.

15.   *O → A and his heirs upon A's marriage.*

(a)   O and A are living; A is unmarried.

16.   *O → B for life, then to C for life, remainder to the heirs of C.*

(a)   B and C are living.

17.   *O → A for life as long as A remains Catholic, then to B and his heirs.*

(a)   A and B are living; A is Catholic.

(b)   A dies.

18.   *O → A for life, then to B and his heirs as long as the land is farmed.*

   (a)   O, A, and B are living; the land is being farmed.

19.   *O → A for life, then to A's firstborn child and that child's heirs.*

   (a)   O and A are living. A has no children.

   (b)   A child is born to A.

20.   *O → A for life, then to B and his heirs, but if B does not marry, then to C and his heirs.*

   (a)   A, B and C are living; B is unmarried.

21.   *O → A for life thirty years from the date of this conveyance.*

   (a)   O and A are living.

   (b)   A dies 29 years later, leaving B as his only heir.

   (c)   One year passes.

22. $O \rightarrow A$ for life, then to B for life, then if C has married W, to C and his heirs.

    (a)   O, A, B, C and W are living; C has not married.

23. $O \rightarrow B$ for life, then if C marries D, to C and her heirs unless C serves liquor on the premises, in which case to E and his heirs.

    (a)   O, B, C, D and E are living; C is unmarried.

24. $O \rightarrow B$ for life, and after B's death, to the heirs of B.

    (a)   O and B are living.

25. $O \rightarrow A$ for life, then to B and his heirs, but if B dies younger than 21, then to C and his heirs.

    (a)   O, A, B and C are living; B is 19.

26. $O \rightarrow A$ for life, then to B and his heirs, but if B dies without children surviving him, then to C and his heirs.

    (a)   O, A, B and C are living; B has five children.

27. $O \rightarrow A$ and his heirs, but if A should marry B, to C and his heirs.

    (a)   A, B and C are living; A has not married B.

28. *O → B for life or until she remarries, then to the heirs of B.*

    (a) The conveyance is in O's will. O is dead. B is O's widow. B is living and has not remarried

29. *O → A for life, then to W for life, then if Z is still alive, to C for life, otherwise to B and his heirs.*

    (a) O, A, W, Z, C and B are living.

30. *O → B for life, remainder to such of B's children as survive B and their heirs.*

    (a) O and B are living; B has no children.

    (b) Triplets, E, F, and G, are born to B.

31. *O → A for life, then to B's heir and his heirs.*

    (a) O, A and B are living.

32. *O → A for life, remainder to B and his heirs, but if B fails to live to 50, then to C and his heirs.*

    (a) A, B and C are living; B is 30.

33. *O → W for life, then to A and his heirs if A survives W, and if A fails to survive W, then to B and his heirs.*

    (a)   O, W, A and B are all living.

    (b)   B dies, without a will, leaving D as his heir.

    (c)   W dies.

    (d)   A dies, without a will, leaving E as his heir.

34. *O → A for life, then if B has married C, to B and his heirs.*

    (a)   O, A, B and C are living; B has not married.

35. *O → A for life, then to B and her heirs if B has married C.*

    (a)   O, A, B and C are living; B has not married.

36. *O → A for life, then if B marries C, to B and her heirs.*

    (a)   O, A, B and C are living; B has not married.

37. *O → A for life, and one year after A's death to B and her heirs.*

    (a)   O, A and B are living.

38. *O → A for life, then to B and his heirs if B writes a complete biography of A's life.*

    (a)   O, A and B are living.

39. *O → A for life, then to B and her heirs after one year.*

    (a)   O, A and B are living.

ANSWER KEY

1.   *Problem:* $O \rightarrow A$ *for life, remainder to B and his heirs if B marries C.*

   Facts: (a)   O, A, B and C are living; B has not married.
   (b)   B marries C.
   (c)   O conveys all his interest to A and her heirs.

   Answer: **Common Law and**
   California, Illinois, Minnesota, New Mexico &
   North Dakota

   (a)   A—life estate
   B—contingent remainder in fee simple
   O—reversion

   (b)   A—life estate
   B—vested remainder in fee simple

   (c)   No change (O has no reversion to convey to A)

2.   *Problem:* $O \rightarrow A$ *for life, then if B has reached the age of 21, to B and his heirs.*

   Facts: (a)   O, A and B are all alive; B is 16.
   (b)   A dies one year later.

   Answer: **Common Law**

   (a)   A—life estate
   B—contingent remainder in fee simple
   O—reversion

   (b)   O—fee simple (B's contingent remainder is destroyed because the supporting estate has expired before his remainder vested)

Answer: **California** (CAL. CIV. CODE § 742)
Illinois (ILL. ANN. STAT. ch. 30, ¶ 40)
Minnesota (MINN. STAT. ANN. § 500.15(3))
North Dakota (N.D. CENT. CODE § 47-02-32)

(a) A—life estate
B—contingent remainder in fee simple
O—reversion

(b) O—fee simple on executory limitation
B—springing executory interest in fee simple

> *Because the doctrine of destructibility of contingent remainders has been abolished, B's interest is not destroyed in this example. For an illustration of a case abolishing the doctrine,* **see ABO Petroleum Corp. v. Amstutz,** *93 N.M. 332, 600 P.2d 278 (1979).*

3. *Problem:* $O \rightarrow A$ for life, then to A's heirs if A survives B.

Facts: O, A and B are living.

Answer: **Common Law**

A—life estate and contingent remainder in fee simple
O—reversion

> *The Rule in* **Shelley's Case** *gave A the remainder which would have gone to the heirs of A. Merger does not apply because A's two estates are not both vested; merger only applies to vested estates.*

Answer: **California** (CAL. CIV. CODE § 779)
Illinois (ILL. ANN. STAT. ch. 30, § 186)
Minnesota (MINN. STAT. ANN. §500.14(4))
New Mexico (N.M. STAT. ANN. § 47-1-19)
North Dakota (N.D. CENT. CODE § 47-04-20)

A—life estate
Heirs of A—contingent remainder in fee simple
O—reversion

Because the Rule in **Shelley's Case** *has been abolished, the heirs of A will take the remainder interest.*

---

4.   *Problem:*   *O → B for life, and one year after B's death to the heirs of B.*

Facts: O and B are living.

Answer: **Common Law** and
California, Illinois, Minnesota, New Mexico & North Dakota

B—life estate
O—reversion in fee simple on executory limitation
heirs of B—springing executory interest in fee simple

The Rule in **Shelley's Case** *does not apply to executory interests, only to remainders.*

---

5. **Problem:** *O → A for life, remainder to B and her heirs if B marries C, and if B does not marry C, to D and his heirs.*

   Facts:
   (a) O, A, B, C and D are living; B has not married.
   (b) B marries C.
   (c) A renounces her life estate.

   Answer: **Common Law** and
   California, Illinois, Minnesota, New Mexico & North Dakota

   (a) A—life estate
   B—contingent remainder in fee simple
   D—alternative contingent remainder in fee simple
   O—reversion

   (b) A—life estate
   B—vested remainder in fee simple

   (c) B—fee simple absolute.

   > *In this case, A's renunciation has the same effect as her death would have had. Here, B had a vested remainder, so there is no question of destruction.*

6. **Problem:** *O → H for life, then to C and his heirs so long as liquor is not sold on the premises.*

   Facts: O, H and C are living.

   Answer: **Common Law** and
   Illinois, Minnesota, New Mexico & North Dakota

   H—life estate
   C—vested remainder in fee simple determinable
   O—possibility of reverter

California (CAL. CIV. CODE § 885.020)

H—life estate
C—vested remainder in fee simple subject to a restriction in
     the form of a condition subsequent
O—power of termination

> *MINN. STAT. ANN. § 500.20(1) provides that a limitation must not be or become merely nominal, and it may be disregarded after 30 years from its creation, § 500.20(2).* **Cf.** *CAL. CIV. CODE § 885.030, which provides expiration dates for powers of termination.*

7. *Problem:*   *O → A for life, then to B and the heirs of his body.*
    Facts: O, A and B are living.

    Answer: **Common Law**

    A—life estate
    B—vested remainder in fee tail
    O—reversion

    Answer: **California** (CAL. CIV. CODE § 763)
                Minnesota (MINN. STAT. ANN. §§ 500.03)
                North Dakota (N.D. CENT. CODE § 47-04-05)

    A—life estate
    B—vested remainder in fee simple
    O—nothing

> *The estate tail has been replaced under these statutes by a fee simple.*

Answer:　　**Illinois** (ILL. ANN. STAT. ch. 30, ¶ 5)
　　　　　　New Mexico (N.M. STAT. ANN. § 47-1-17)

　　　　A—life estate
　　　　B—vested remainder in a life estate
　　　　Children of B (if born)—vested remainder, subject to open, in
　　　　　　fee simple
　　　　Children of B (if not born)—contingent remainder in fee
　　　　　　simple
　　　　O—reversion

> *The estate tail has been replaced under these statutes by a life estate and remainder in fee.*

8.　　*Problem:*　　$O \rightarrow A$.

　　　Facts:　　O and A are living.

　　　Answer:　　**Common Law**

　　　　A—life estate
　　　　O—reversion

　　　　California (CAL. CIV. CODE § 1105)
　　　　Illinois (ILL. ANN. STAT. ch. 30, ¶ 12)
　　　　Minnesota (MINN. STAT. ANN. § 500.02)
　　　　New Mexico (N.M. STAT. ANN. § 47-1-33)
　　　　North Dakota (N.D. CENT. CODE § 47-10-13)

　　　　A—fee simple

> *Words of inheritance are unnecessary under most modern statutory schemes.*

9. ***Problem:*** *O → A for life, then to A's children and their heirs.*

    Facts:
    (a) O and A are living. A has no children.
    (b) One child, C, is born to A.

    Answer: **Common Law** and
    California, Illinois, Minnesota, New Mexico & North Dakota

    (a) A—life estate
        Children of A—contingent remainder in fee simple
        O—reversion

    (b) A—life estate
        C—vested remainder, subject to open, in fee simple

10. ***Problem:*** *O → A for life, then to B's heirs.*

    Facts: O, A and B are living.

    Answer: **Common Law** and
    California, Illinois, Minnesota, New Mexico & North Dakota

    A—life estate
    Heir of B—contingent remainder in fee simple
    O—reversion

    > *The phrase "to B's heirs" is read "to B's heir and his heirs." Even if B has children, the remainder is contingent because no one knows who B's heir will be until B dies. An heir is determined at the time of B's death. Also, the Rule in* **Shelley's Case** *does not apply, since the grant of a remainder is not to the heirs of the life tenant.*

11. **Problem:** *O → A until she dies.*

 Facts: O and A are living.

 Answer: **Common Law** and
 California, Illinois, Minnesota, New Mexico & North Dakota

 A—life estate
 O—reversion

12. **Problem:** *O → A and the heirs of his body, then to the children of B and their heirs.*

 Facts: (a) O, A and B are living; A and B have no children; A is married, and B is married.
 (b) A has a child, C.
 (c) B has a child, D.
 (d) B dies.
 (e) A dies with a will leaving all his property to F and his heirs.

 Answer: **Common Law**

 (a) A—fee tail
 Children of B—contingent remainder in fee simple
 O—reversion

 (b) no change

 (c) A—fee tail
 D—vested remainder, subject to open, in fee simple

 (d) A—fee tail
 D—vested remainder in fee simple (no longer subject to open)

 (e) C—fee tail
 D—vested remainder in fee simple

Answer: **California** (CAL. CIV. CODE §§ 763, 764)
              North Dakota (N.D. CENT. CODE §§ 47-04-05, 06)

(a)   A—fee simple on executory limitation
        Children of B—executory interest in fee

(b)   no change

(c)   A—fee simple on executory limitation
        D—executory interest in fee

(d)   A—fee simple on executory limitation
        D—executory interest in fee

(e)   F—fee simple

> *This future interest is statutorily created; we substituted the common law terms that seem most consistent with the statutory description.*

Answer: **Illinois** (ILL. ANN. STAT. ch. 30, ¶ 5)
              New Mexico (N.M. STAT. ANN. § 47-1-17)

(a)   A—life estate
        Children of A—contingent remainder in fee simple
        Children of B—alternative contingent remainder in
             fee simple
        O—reversion

(b)   A—life estate
        C—vested remainder, subject to open, in fee simple

(c)   no change

(d)   no change

(e)   C—fee simple

Answer: **Minnesota** (MINN. STAT. ANN. §§ 500.03, 04)

(a)   A—fee simple absolute

(b)   no change

(c)   no change

(d)   no change

(e)   F—fee simple absolute

> **But see Buel v. Southwick**, *70 N.Y. 581 (1877). In that case a similar statute, clear on its face, was held not to destroy a remainder following the "fee tail."*

13.   *Problem:*   *O → C for life, remainder to B for life, then to the heirs of B.*

Facts: (a)   O, B and C are all alive.

Answer: **Common Law**

C—life estate
B—vested remainder in fee simple.
O—nothing

> *The Rule in* **Shelley's Case** *vests the second remainder in B. The two vested remainders then merge.*

Answer: **California** (CAL. CIV. CODE § 779)
Illinois (ILL. ANN. STAT. ch. 30, ¶ 186)
Minnesota (MINN. STAT. ANN. § 500.14(4))
New Mexico (N.M. STAT. ANN. § 47-1-19)
North Dakota (N.D. CENT. CODE § 47-04-20)

C—life estate
B—vested remainder in a life estate
Heirs of B—contingent remainder in fee simple
O—reversion

> *The Rule in* **Shelley's Case** *has been abolished.*

14. *Problem:* *O → B for life, remainder to C for life, then to the heirs of B.*

Facts: (a) O, B and C are all alive.
(b) C dies.

Answer: **Common Law**

(a) B—life estate and a vested remainder in fee simple
C—vested remainder in a life estate

> *Rule in* **Shelley's Case**. *Merger does not apply because of the intervening vested remainder.*

(b) B—fee simple absolute.

> *C's remainder was vested, but only for life, so it disappears. B's interests then merge.*

Answer: **California** (CAL. CIV. CODE § 779)
Illinois (ILL. ANN. STAT. ch. 30, ¶ 186)
Minnesota (MINN. STAT. ANN. § 500.14(4))
New Mexico (N.M. STAT. ANN. § 47-1-19)
North Dakota (N.D. CENT. CODE § 47-04-20)

(a)   B—life estate
C—vested remainder in a life estate
Heirs of B—contingent remainder in fee simple
O—reversion

(b)   B—life estate
Heirs of B—contingent remainder in fee simple
O—reversion

> *The Rule in* **Shelley's Case** *has been abolished.*

15.   *Problem:* $O \rightarrow A$ *and his heirs upon A's marriage.*

Facts: O and A are living; A is unmarried.

Answer: **Common Law** and
California, Illinois, Minnesota, New Mexico & North Dakota

O—fee simple on executory limitation
A—springing executory interest in fee simple

> *If you thought A had a fee simple determinable ... A does not have a present interest. The present interest is held by O, who will not give it up until A is married. In fact, if A never marries, O retains a fee simple. A has only a future interest. If you thought O had a fee simple determinable ... you have correctly understood the practical aspect of O's interest, but the form is not right for a fee simple determinable.*

16. *Problem:* O → B for life, then to C for life, remainder to the heirs of C.

Facts: B and C are living.

Answer: **Common Law**

B—life estate
C—vested remainder in fee simple

> *The example illustrates the Rule in **Shelley's Case** and merger. The Rule operates even though C's interest is a future interest, not presently possessory.*

Answer: **California** (CAL. CIV. CODE § 779)
Illinois (ILL. ANN. STAT. ch. 30, ¶ 186)
Minnesota (MINN. STAT. ANN. § 500.14(4))
New Mexico (N.M. STAT. ANN. § 47-1-19)
North Dakota (N.D. CENT. CODE §§ 47-04-20)

B—life estate
C—vested remainder in life estate
Heirs of C—contingent remainder in fee simple
O—reversion

> *The Rule in* **Shelley's Case** *has been abolished.*

17. **Problem:** O → A for life as long as A remains Catholic, then to B and his heirs.

    Facts:
    (a) A and B are living; A is Catholic.
    (b) A dies.

    Answer: **Common Law** and
    California, Illinois, Minnesota, New Mexico & North Dakota

    (a) A—life estate determinable
        B—vested remainder in fee simple

    > *There is some difference of opinion here. See the explanatory note to Problem 28,* **infra**.

    (b) B—fee simple

18. **Problem:** O → A for life, then to B and his heirs as long as the land is farmed.

    Facts: O, A and B are living; the land is being farmed.

    Answer: **Common Law** and
    Illinois, Minnesota, New Mexico & North Dakota

    A—life estate
    B—vested remainder in fee simple determinable
    O—possibility of reverter

> *Why vested? B takes when A dies, and can only lose the land if he subsequently fails to farm the land. There is no condition on his taking of the land upon A's death; i.e., on his right to acquire possession. In fact, even if A didn't farm the land, B gets it.* **Cf.** *Problem 6.*

California (CAL. CIV. CODE § 885.020)

A—life estate

B—vested remainder in fee simple subject to a restriction in the form of a condition subsequent

O—power of termination

> *MINN. STAT. ANN. § 500.20(1) provides that a limitation must not be or become merely nominal, and it may be disregarded after 30 years from its creation, § 500.20(2).* **Cf.** *CAL. CIV. CODE § 885.030, which provides expiration dates for powers of termination.*

19.   ***Problem:***   *O → A for life, then to A's firstborn child and that child's heirs.*

   Facts:
(a)   O and A are living. A has no children.
(b)   A child is born to A.

   Answer: **Common Law** and
California, Illinois, Minnesota, New Mexico & North Dakota

(a)   A—life estate
1st child of A—contingent remainder in fee simple
O—reversion

(b)   A—life estate
1st child of A—vested remainder in fee simple

> *Once A's first child is born, the remainder becomes vested in her or him.*

20. **Problem:** *O → A for life, then to B and his heirs, but if B does not marry, then to C and his heirs.*

Facts: A, B and C are living; B is unmarried.

Answer: **Common Law** and
California, Illinois, Minnesota, New Mexico & North Dakota

A—life estate
B—vested remainder, subject to divestment, in fee
C—shifting executory interest in fee simple

> *See the answer to review problem 4, at the end of Chapter Four, supra.*

21. **Problem:** *O → A for life thirty years from the date of this conveyance.*

Facts:
(a)   O and A are living.
(b)   A dies 29 years later, leaving B as his only heir.
(c)   One year passes.

Answer: **Common Law** and
California, Illinois, Minnesota, New Mexico & North Dakota

(a)   O—fee simple on executory limitation, and a reversion in fee
      A—springing executory interest in a life estate
(b)   O—fee simple
(c)   No change

22. **Problem:** $O \rightarrow A$ *for life, then to B for life, then if C has married W, to C and his heirs.*

Facts: O, A, B, C and W are living; C has not married.

Answer: **Common Law** and
California, Illinois, Minnesota, New Mexico & North Dakota

A—life estate
B—vested remainder in life estate
C—contingent remainder in fee simple
O—reversion

23. **Problem:** $O \rightarrow B$ *for life, then if C marries D, to C and his heirs unless C serves liquor on the premises, in which case to E and his heirs.*

Facts: O, B, C, D and E are living; C is unmarried.

Answer: **Common Law** and
Illinois, Minnesota, New Mexico & North Dakota

B—life estate
C—contingent remainder in fee simple on executory
limitation
E—shifting executory interest in fee simple
O—reversion

> *Suppose C does not marry D—then the land reverts to O.*

California (CAL. CIV. CODE § 885.10(a)(2)

The foregoing answer is probably still correct, but because the definition of a power of termination encompasses an executory interest created in a transferee to enforce a restriction on use, it also would seem appropriate to describe E's interest as a power of termination.

24. **Problem:** *O → B for life, and after B's death to the heirs of B.*

Facts: O and B are living.

Answer: **Common Law**

B—fee simple absolute

> *In this example, because of the Rule in* **Shelley's Case***, B has a life estate and a vested remainder in fee simple, rather than B's heirs having a contingent remainder in fee simple. Then, under the doctrine of merger, B's life estate and remainder became a present fee simple.*

Answer: **California** (CAL. CIV. CODE § 779)
Illinois (ILL. ANN. STAT. ch. 30, ¶ 186)
Minnesota (MINN. STAT. ANN. § 500.14(4))
New Mexico (N.M. STAT. ANN. § 47-1-19)
North Dakota (N.D. CENT. CODE § 47-04-20)

B—life estate
Heirs of B—contingent remainder in fee simple
O—reversion

> *The Rule in* **Shelley's Case** *has been abolished.*

25. **Problem:** *O → A for life, then to B and his heirs, but if B dies younger than 21, then to C and his heirs.*

Facts: O, A, B and C are living. B is 19.

Answer: **Common Law** and
California, Illinois, Minnesota, New Mexico & North Dakota

A—life estate
B—vested remainder, subject to divestment, in fee
C—shifting executory interest in fee simple

> *See the answer to Review Problem 4, at the end of Chapter Four,*
> **supra***; cf. Problem 20,* **supra***.*

26. **Problem:** *O → A for life, then to B and his heirs, but if B dies without children surviving him, then to C and his heirs.*

Facts: O, A, B and C are living; B has 5 children.

Answer: **Common Law** and
California, Illinois, Minnesota, New Mexico & North Dakota

A—life estate
B—vested remainder, subject to divestment, in fee
C—shifting executory interest in fee simple

> *See the answer to Review Problem 4, at the end of Chapter Four,*
> **supra***; cf. Problem 20,* **supra***.*

27. **Problem:** *O → A and his heirs, but if A should marry B, to C and his heirs.*

Facts: A, B and C are living. A has not married B.

Answer: **Common Law** and
California, Illinois, Minnesota, New Mexico

A—fee simple on executory limitation
C—shifting executory interest in fee simple

> *C's interest does not satisfy the requirements of a remainder because it may, if A marries B, cut short A's interest.*

North Dakota (N.D. CENT. CODE § 47-02-25)

A—fee simple (you might have added that if there was more evidence of O's intent, the grant might have been valid under the statute. If so, A would have a fee simple on executory limitation and C would have a shifting executory interest in fee)

28. **Problem:** *O → B for life or until she remarries, then to the heirs of B.*

Facts: The conveyance is in O's will. O is dead. B is O's widow. B is living and has not remarried.

Answer: **Common Law**

B—fee simple

> *The Rule in **Shelley's Case** gives B both a life estate determinable and a vested remainder in fee simple; merger converts these into a present fee simple.*

Answer: **California** (CAL. CIV. CODE § 779)
                 Illinois (ILL. ANN. STAT. ch. 30, ¶ 186)
                 Minnesota (MINN. STAT. ANN. § 500.14(4))
                 New Mexico (N.M. STAT. ANN. § 47-1-19)
                 North Dakota (N.D. CENT. CODE §§ 47-02-25, 47-04-20)

B—life estate determinable
Heirs of B—contingent remainder in fee simple
O—reversion

The Rule in **Shelley's Case** *has been abolished, so the phrase "to the heirs of B" is not rewritten. Those heirs will not be determined until B's death; hence, the remainder is contingent.*

That the future interest is a remainder was explained in Chapter Six. However, the explanation there was somewhat simplified, as discussed in this excerpt of a letter written on April 19, 1980, by Professor Laurence to Professor Beverly A. Rowlett, then of the University of Tennessee College of Law, April 9, 1980:

> *It was nice to talk to you earlier today. I'm sorry I didn't have the answer at hand. Our authority for the answer to problem 28 is 1 Simes and Smith § 107. They cite 2 Restatement of Property § 156, Illustration 6. Both of these sources support our position exactly. The authority they cite, however, is dicta:* **Seay v. Seay**, *384 S.W.2d 466, 238 Ark. 808 (1964),* **Conger v. Conger**, *494 P.2d 1081, 208 Kan. 823 (1972).*

> *The distinction between these sources and those cited by Professor Sewell seems to be between the interest following a life estate determinable (O →A for life until he doesn't pay the taxes, then to B and his heirs;* **Seay**) *and one following a life estate subject to an executory interest (O →A for life, but if A becomes insolvent, then to B and his heirs;* **Blackman v. Fysh**, *[1892] 3 Ch. 209). The difference is, I guess, that the life estate determinable naturally expires when the condition is broken, while the "but if ..." language of the other estate is seen to cut short the life estate. Hence, a remainder would follow the former and an executory interest the latter. This is consistent with the dicta in* **Seay** *and* **Conger**.

> *It is consistent also, I think, with our discussion in the text. I now see that that explanation, as with so much else in the Student's Guide, is an oversimplification. We can live with that, I think, although a cite to Simes & Smith probably ought to be there.*

> *That's all the news. I will be interested in your colleague's reaction, if any, to this letter.*

29.   *Problem:*   *O → A for life, then to W for life, then if Z is still alive, to C for life, otherwise to B and his heirs.*

Facts: O, A, W, Z, C and B are living.

Answer: **Common Law** and
California, Illinois, Minnesota, New Mexico & North Dakota

A—life estate
W—vested remainder in life estate
C—contingent remainder in life estate (not ***pur autre vie***
      because it is only contingent on Z's being alive at the
      time of W's death; it is not measured by anyone's
      life other than C's)
B—alternative contingent remainder in fee simple
O—reversion

30.   *Problem:*   *O → B for life, remainder to such of B's children as survive B and their heirs.*

Facts: (a)   O and B are living. B has no children.
            (b)   Triplets, E, F and G, are born to B.

Answer: **Common Law** and
California, Illinois, Minnesota, New Mexico & North Dakota

(a)   B—life estate
      Children of B who survive B—contingent remainder
            in fee simple
      O—reversion

(b)   same as (a) because even though E, F and G are alive
            now, they must fulfill the condition of being
            alive when B dies, so their remainder is still
            contingent

31.   *Problem:*   *O → A for life, then to B's heir and his heirs.*

   Facts: O, A and B are living.

   Answer: **Common Law** and
   **California, Illinois, Minnesota, New Mexico &
         North Dakota**

   A—life estate
   Heir of B—contingent remainder in fee simple
   O—reversion

   > *The remainder is contingent because a living person has no heir. The
   > Rule in* **Shelley's Case** *does not apply because the remainder was not
   > granted to the life tenant's heirs.*

32.   *Problem:*   *O → A for life, remainder to B and his heirs, but if B fails to
         live to 50, then to C and his heirs.*
   Facts: A, B and C are living; B is 30.

   Answer: **Common Law** and
   **California, Illinois, Minnesota, New Mexico &
         North Dakota**

   A—life estate
   B—vested remainder, subject to divestment, in fee
   C—shifting executory interest in fee simple

   > *See the answer to review problem 4, at the end of Chapter Two,*
   > **supra***; cf. Problem 20,* **supra***.*

33.   **Problem:**   *O → W for life, then to A and his heirs if A survives W, and if A fails to survive W, then to B and his heirs.*

    Facts:
- (a)   O, W, A and B are all living.
- (b)   B dies, without a will, leaving D as his heir.
- (c)   W dies.
- (d)   A dies, without a will, leaving E as his heir.

    Answer: **Common Law** and
California, Illinois, Minnesota, New Mexico & North Dakota

- (a)   W—life estate
A—contingent remainder in fee simple
B—alternative contingent remainder in fee simple
O—reversion

- (b)   same as (a) except D has B's alternative contingent remainder

- (c)   A—fee simple absolute

> *A has met the condition of surviving W, so A takes the estate.*

- (d)   E—fee simple absolute

34.   **Problem:**   *O → A for life, then if B has married C, to B and his heirs.*

    Facts: O, A, B and C are living; B has not married.

    Answer: **Common Law** and
California, Illinois, Minnesota, New Mexico & North Dakota

A—life estate
B—contingent remainder in fee simple
O—reversion

35. **Problem:**   *O → A for life, then to B and her heirs if B has married C.*

    Facts: O, A, B and C are living; B has not married.

    Answer: **Common Law** and
    California, Illinois, Minnesota, New Mexico &
    North Dakota

    A—life estate
    B—contingent remainder in fee simple
    O—reversion

    > *The difference in language,* **cf**. *Problem 34, does not change the classification. The "if B has married C" clause is still a condition precedent. If B marries C before A dies, A's life estate is not cut off. B's interest would merely become vested.*

36. **Problem:**   *O → A for life, then if B marries C, to B and her heirs.*

    Facts: O, A, B and C are living; B has not married.

    Answer: **Common Law** and
    California, Illinois, Minnesota, New Mexico &
    North Dakota

    A—life estate
    B—contingent remainder in fee simple
    O—reversion

    > *Case law (***Purefoy v. Rogers***, discussed in connection with the Statute of Uses) interprets "if B marries C" to mean "if B has married C." Thus, the marriage can take place before A's death and still meet the condition. In fact, if B marries C before A's death, B's contingent remainder becomes vested. Even after the Statute of Uses, an interest was construed as a contingent remainder rather than an executory interest if the interest had the capacity to operate as a contingent remainder. Suppose that A dies before B marries C. In 1700, B's contingent remainder would be destroyed.*

37.   *Problem:* $O \rightarrow A$ *for life, and one year after A's death, to B and her heirs.*

   Facts: O, A and B are living.

   Answer: **Common Law** and
   California, Illinois, Minnesota, New Mexico &
   North Dakota

   A—life estate
   O—reversion (in fee simple on executory limitation)
   B—springing executory interest in fee simple

   The material in parentheses frequently is omitted.

38.   *Problem:* $O \rightarrow A$ *for life, then to B and his heirs if B writes a complete biography of A's life.*

   Facts: O, A and B are living.

   Answer: **Common Law** and
   California, Illinois, Minnesota, New Mexico &
   North Dakota

   A—life estate
   O—reversion (in fee simple on executory limitation)
   B—springing executory interest in fee simple

   B couldn't be ready to take immediately upon A's death, since it takes a while to write a complete biography. A complete biography includes an account of the subject's death.

39. **Problem:**   *O → A for life, then to B and her heirs after one year.*

Facts: O, A and B are living.

Answer: **Common Law** and
**California, Illinois, Minnesota, New Mexico &
       North Dakota**

A—life estate
O—reversion (in fee simple on executory limitation)
B—springing executory interest in fee simple

O's future interest is in a possessory estate that is subject to an executory interest, because of the "one year" condition. B's interest was not possible before 1536. After 1536, it can be created, as an executory interest.

APPENDIX III

SELECTED STATUTES

A. CALIFORNIA

1. Civil Code

§ 683. *Joint tenancy; definition; method of creation*

(a) A joint interest is one owned by two or more persons in equal shares, by a title created by a single will or transfer, when expressly declared in the will or transfer to be a joint tenancy, or by transfer from a sole owner to himself or herself and others, or from tenants in common or joint tenants to themselves or some of them, or to themselves or any of them and others, or from a husband and wife, when holding title as community property or otherwise to themselves or to themselves and others or to one of them and to another or others, when expressly declared in the transfer to be a joint tenancy, or when granted or devised to executors or trustees as joint tenants. A joint tenancy in personal property may be created by a written transfer, instrument or agreement.

(b) Provisions of this section do not apply to a joint account in a financial institution if Part 2 (commencing with Section 5100) of Division 5 of the Probate Code applies to such account.

§ 686. *Interest in common; interests excluded*

Every interest created in favor of several persons in their own right is an interest in common, unless acquired by them in partnership, for partnership purposes, or unless declared in its creation to be a joint interest, as provided in Section 683, or unless acquired as community property.

§ 741. *Future interests; alienation or loss of precedent interest*

No future interest can be defeated or barred by any alienation or other act of the owner of the intermediate or precedent interest, nor by any destruction of such precedent interest by forfeiture, surrender, merger, or otherwise, except as provided by the next section, or where a forfeiture is imposed by statute as a penalty for the violation thereof.

§ 742. *Future interests; premature determination of precedent interest*

No future interest, valid in its creation, is defeated by the determination of the precedent interest before the happening of the contingency on which the future interest is limited to take effect; but should such contingency afterwards happen, the future interest takes effect in the same manner and to the same extent as if the precedent interest had continued to the same period.

§ 763. *Estates tail abolished; fee simple and fee simple absolute*

Estates tail are abolished, and every estate which would be at common law adjudged to be a fee tail is a fee simple; and if no valid remainder is limited thereon, is a fee simple absolute.

§ 764. *Fee tails as contingent remainders*

Where a remainder in fee is limited upon any estate, which would by the common law be adjudged a fee tail, such remainder is valid as a contingent limitation upon a fee, and vests in possession on the death of the first taker, without issue living at the time of his death.

§ 779. *Heirs of life purchasers; taking as purchasers*

When a remainder is limited to the heirs, or heirs of the body, of a person to whom a life estate in the same property is given, the persons who, on the termination of the life estate, are the successors or heirs of the body of the owner for life, are entitled to take by virtue of the remainder so limited to them, and not as mere successors of the owner for life.

§ 885.010. *Definitions*

(a) As used in this chapter

(1) "Power of termination" means the power to terminate a fee simple estate in real property to enforce a restriction in the form of a condition subsequent to which the fee simple estate is subject, whether the power is characterized in the instrument that creates or evidences it as a power of termination, right of entry or reentry, right of possession or repossession, reserved power of revocation, or otherwise, and includes a possibility of reverter that is deemed to be and is enforceable as a power of termination pursuant to Section 885.020.

(2) "Power of termination" includes the power created in a transferee to terminate a fee simple estate in real property to enforce a restriction on the use of the real property in the form of a limitation or condition subsequent to which the fee simple estate is subject, whether the power is characterized in the instrument that creates or evidences it as an executory interest, executory limitation, or otherwise, and includes the interest known at common law as an executory interest preceded by a fee simple determinable.

(b) A power of termination is an interest in the real property.

(c) For the purpose of applying this chapter to other statutes relating to powers of termination, the terms "right of reentry," "right of repossession for a breach of condition subsequent," and comparable terms used in the other statutes mean "power of termination" as defined in this section.

§ 885.020. *Fees simple determinable and possibilities of reverter abolished*

Fees simple determinable and possibilities of reverter are abolished. Every estate that would be at common law a fee simple determinable is deemed to be a fee simple subject to a restriction in the form of a condition subsequent. Every interest that would be at common law a possibility of reverter is deemed to be and is enforceable as a power of termination.

§ 885.030. *Expiration dates; recorded instruments; contrary provisions*

(a)   A power of termination of record expires at the later of the following times:

(1)   Thirty years after the date the instrument reserving, transferring, or otherwise evidencing the power of termination is recorded.

(2)   Thirty years after the date a notice of intent to preserve the power of termination is recorded, if the notice is recorded within the time prescribed in paragraph (1).

(3)   Thirty years after the date an instrument reserving, transferring, or otherwise evidencing the power of termination or a notice of intent to preserve the power of termination is recorded, if the instrument or notice is recorded within 30 years after the date such an instrument or notice was last recorded.

(b)   This section applies notwithstanding any provision to the contrary in the instrument reserving, transferring or otherwise evidencing the power of termination or in another recorded document unless the instrument or other recorded document provides an earlier expiration date.

§ 885.040. *Obsolete powers; expiration; grants to public entities, etc.*

(a)   If a power of termination becomes obsolete, the power expires.

(b)   As used in this section, a power of termination is obsolete if any of the following circumstances applies:

(1)   The restriction to which the fee simple estate is subject is of no actual and substantial benefit to the holder of the power.

(2)   Enforcement of the power would not effectuate the purpose of the restriction to which the fee simple estate is subject.

(3)   It would be otherwise inequitable to enforce the power because of changed conditions or circumstances.

(c)   No power of termination shall expire under this section during the life of the grantor if it arises from a grant by a natural person without consideration to a public entity or to a society, corporation, institution, or association exempt by the laws of this state from taxation.

§ 1071. *Definitions; heirs; issue*

Where a future interest is limited by a grant to take effect on the death of any person without heirs, or heirs of his body, or without issue, or in equivalent words, such words must be taken to mean successors, or issue living at the death of the person named as ancestor.

§ 1072. *Words of inheritance or succession*

Words of inheritance or succession are not requisite to transfer a fee in real property.

§ 1073. *Conveyance to grantor's own heirs or next of kin*

The law of this State does not include (1) the common law rule of worthier title that a grantor cannot convey an interest to his own heirs or (2) a presumption or rule of interpretation that a grantor does not intend, by a grant to his own heirs or next of kin, to transfer an interest to them. The meaning of a grant of a legal or equitable interest to a grantor's own heirs or next of kin, however designated, shall be determined by the general rules applicable to the interpretation of grants. This section shall be applied in all cases in which final judgment has not been entered on its effective date.

§ 1105. *Fee simple title; presumption*

A fee simple title is presumed to pass by a grant of real property, unless it appears from the grant that a lesser estate was intended.

2. Probate Code

§ 6145. *Common law rule of worthier title; devise of interest to testator's own heirs or next of kin*

The law of this state does not include (1) the common law rule of worthier title that a testator cannot devise an interest to his or her own heirs or (2) a presumption or rule of interpretation that a testator does not intend, by a devise to his or her own heirs or next of kin, to transfer an interest to them. The meaning of a devise of a legal or equitable interest to a testator's own heirs or next of kin, however designated, shall be determined by the general rules applicable to the interpretation of wills. This section applies to all cases in which a final judgment had not been entered as of September 18, 1959.

§ 21200. *Short title*

This chapter shall be known and may be cited as the Uniform Statutory Rule Against Perpetuities.

§ 21201. *Common law rule superseded*

This chapter supersedes the common law rule against perpetuities.

§ 21202. *Application of part*

(a)   Except as provided in subdivision (b), this part applies to nonvested property interests and unexercised powers of appointment regardless of whether they were created before, on, or after January 1, 1992.

(b)   This part does not apply to any property interest or power of appointment the validity of which has been determined in a judicial proceeding or by a settlement among interested persons.

§ 21205. *Nonvested property interests; validity; conditions*

A nonvested property interest is invalid unless one of the following conditions is satisfied:

(a)   When the interest is created, it is certain to vest or terminate no later than 21 years after the death of an individual then alive.

(b)   The interest either vests or terminates within 90 years after its creation.

§ 21208. *Posthumous births*

In determining whether a nonvested property interest or a power of appointment is valid under this article, the possibility that a child will be born to an individual after the individual's death is disregarded.

§ 21209. *Construction of "later of" language in perpetuity saving clause; application of section*

(a)   If, in measuring a period from the creation of a trust or other property arrangement, language in a governing instrument (1) seeks to disallow the vesting or termination of any interest or trust beyond, (2) seeks to postpone the vesting or termination of any interest or trust until, or (3) seeks to operate in effect in any similar fashion upon, the later of (A) the expiration of a period of time not exceeding 21 years after the death of the survivor of specified lives in being at the creation of the trust or other property arrangement or (B) the expiration of a period of time that exceeds or might exceed 21 years after the death of the survivor of lives in being at the creation of the trust or other property arrangement, that language is inoperative to the extent it produces a period that exceeds 21 years after the death of the survivor of the specified lives.

(b)   Notwithstanding Section 21202, this section applies only to governing instruments, including instruments exercising powers of appointment, executed on or after January 1, 1992.

§ 21220. *Petition; conditions*

On petition of an interested party, a court shall reform a disposition in the manner that most closely approximates the transferor's manifested plan of distribution and is within the 90 years allowed by the applicable provision in Article 2 (commencing with Section 21205), if any of the following conditions is satisfied:

(a)   A nonvested property interest or a power of appointment becomes invalid under the statutory rule against perpetuities provided in Article 2 (commencing with Section 21205).

(b)   A class gift is not but might become invalid under the statutory rule against perpetuities provided in Article 2 (commencing with Section 21205), and the time has arrived when the share of any class member is to take effect in possession or enjoyment.

(c)   A nonvested property interest that is not validated by subdivision (a) of Section 21205 can vest but not with 90 years after its creation.

§ 21225. *Application of chapter*

This chapter does not apply to any of the following:

(a)   A nonvested property interest or a power of appointment arising out of a nondonative transfer, except a nonvested property interest or a power of appointment arising out of (1) a premarital or postmarital agreement, (2) a separation or divorce settlement, (3) a spouse's election, (4) or a similar arrangement arising out of a prospective, existing, or previous marital relationship between the parties, (5) a contract to make or not to revoke a will or trust, (6) a contract to exercise or not to exercise a power of appointment, (7) a transfer in satisfaction of a duty of support, or (8) a reciprocal transfer.

(b)   A fiduciary's power relating to the administration or management of assets, including the power of a fiduciary to sell, lease, or mortgage property, and the power of a fiduciary to determine principal and income.

(c)   A power to appoint a fiduciary.

(d)   A discretionary power of a trustee to distribute principal before termination of a trust to a beneficiary having an indefeasibly vested interest in the income and principal.

(e)   A nonvested property interest held by charity, government, or governmental agency or subdivision, if the nonvested property interest is preceded by an interest held by another charity, government, or governmental agency or subdivision.

(f)   A nonvested property interest in or a power of appointment with respect to a trust or other property arrangement forming part of a pension, profit-sharing, stock bonus, health, disability, death benefit, income deferral, or other current or deferred benefit plan for one or more employees, independent contractors, or their beneficiaries or spouses, to which contributions are made for the purpose of distributing to or for the benefit of the participants or their beneficiaries or spouses the property, income, or principal in the trust or other property arrangement, except a nonvested property interest or a power of appointment that is created by an election of a participant or a beneficiary or spouse.

(g)   A property interest, power of appointment, or arrangement that was not subject to the common law rule against perpetuities or is excluded by another statute of this state.

(h)   A trust created for the purpose of providing for its beneficiaries under hospital service contracts, group life insurance, group disability insurance, group annuities, or any combination of such insurance, as defined in the Insurance Code.

§ 21230. *Validating lives*

The lives of individuals selected to govern the time of vesting pursuant to Article 2 (commencing with Section 21205) of Chapter 1 may not be so numerous or so situated that evidence of their deaths is likely to be unreasonably difficult to obtain.

§ 21231. *Spouse as life in being*

In determining the validity of a nonvested property interest pursuant to Article 2 (commencing with Section 21205) of Chapter 1, an individual described as the spouse of an individual alive at the commencement of the perpetuities period shall be deemed to be an individual alive when the interest is created, whether or not the individual so described was then alive.

B.   ILLINOIS

1.   Chapter 30

¶ 5.   *Entailment*

§ 6. In cases where, by the common law, any person or persons might hereafter become the owner of, without applying the rule of property known as the rule in Shelley's Case, in fee tail, of any lands, tenements or hereditaments, by virtue of any legacy, gift, grant or other conveyance, hereafter to be made, or by any other means whatsoever, such person or persons, instead of being or becoming the owner thereof in fee tail, shall be deemed and adjudged to be, and become the owner thereof, for his or her natural life only, and the remainder shall pass in fee simple absolute, to the person or persons to whom the estate tail would, on the death of the first grantee, legatee or donee in tail, first pass, according to the course of the common law, by virtue of such legacy, gift, grant or conveyance.

¶ 12.   *What estate conveyed*

§ 13. Every estate in lands which shall be granted, conveyed or bequeathed, although other words heretofore necessary to transfer an estate of inheritance is not added, shall be deemed a fee simple estate of inheritance, if a less estate is not limited by express words, or do not appear to have been granted, conveyed or bequeathed by construction or operation of law.

¶ 37e.   *Duration of possibility of reverter or rights of entry or re-entry for breach of condition*

Neither possibilities of reverter nor rights of entry or re-entry for breach of condition subsequent, whether heretofore or hereafter created, where the condition has not been broken, shall be valid for a longer period than 40 years from the date of the creation of the condition or possibility of reverter. If such a possibility of reverter or right of entry or re-entry is created to endure for a longer period than 40 years, it shall be valid for 40 years.

¶ 39. *Surrender or merger of reversion*

§ 1. When the reversion expectant on a lease, made either before or after the passing of this act, of tenements or hereditaments of any tenure, shall be surrendered or merged, the estate, which shall for the time being confer as against the tenant under the same lease the next vested right to the same tenements or hereditaments, shall, to the extent and for the purpose of preserving such incidents to, and obligations on the same reversion, as but for the surrender or merger thereof, would have subsisted, be deemed the reversion expectant on the same lease.

¶ 40. *When not defeated*

§ 1. No future interest shall fail or be defeated by the determination of any precedent estate or interest prior to the happening of the event or contingency on which the future interest is limited to take effect.

¶ 186. *Abolition of rule*

The rule of property known as the rule in Shelley's Case is abolished.

¶ 188. *Abolition of worthier title and of rule that grantor cannot create limitations in favor of own heirs*

Where a deed, will or other instrument purports to create any present or future interest in real or personal property in the heirs of the maker of the instrument, the heirs shall take, by purchase and not by descent, the interest that the instrument purports to create. The doctrine of worthier title and the rule of the common law that a grantor cannot create a limitation in favor of his own heirs are abolished.

¶ **192.** *Purpose*

§ 2. Purpose. This Act modifies the common law rule of property known as the rule against perpetuities, which, except as modified by statutes in force at the effective date of this Act and by this Act, shall remain in full force and effect.

¶ **194.** *Application of the rule against perpetuities*

§ 4.　(a)　[Omitted]

(b)　The period of the rule against perpetuities shall not commence to run in connection with any disposition of property or interest therein, and no instrument shall be regarded as becoming effective for purposes of the rule against perpetuities, and no interest or power shall be deemed to be created for purposes of the rule against perpetuities as long as, by the terms of the instrument, the maker of the instrument has the power to revoke the instrument or to transfer or direct to be transferred to himself the entire legal and equitable ownership of the property or interest therein.

(c)　In determining whether an interest violates the rule against perpetuities:

(1)　It shall be presumed (A) that the interest was intended to be valid, (B) in the case of an interest conditioned upon the probate of a will, the appointment of an executor, administrator or trustee, the completion of the administration of an estate, the payment of debts, the sale or distribution of property, the determination of federal or state tax liabilities or the happening of any administrative contingency, that the contingency must occur, if at all, within the period of the rule against perpetuities, and (C) where the instrument creates an interest in the "widow," "widower," or "spouse" of another person, that the maker of the instrument intended to refer to a person who was living at the date that the period of the rule against perpetuities commences to run;

(2)　where any interest, but for this subparagraph (c) (2), would be invalid because it is made to depend upon any person attaining or failing to attain an age in excess of 21 years, the age specified shall be reduced to 21 years as to every person to whom the age contingency applies;

　　　　　　　(3)　　if, notwithstanding the provisions of subparagraphs (c) (1) and (2) of this Section, the validity of any interest depends upon the possibility of the birth or adoption of a child, (A) no person shall be deemed capable of having a child until he has attained the age of 13 years, (B) any person who has attained the age of 65 years shall be deemed incapable of having a child, (C) evidence shall be admissible as to the incapacity of having a child by a living person who has not attained the age of 65 years, and (D) the possibility of having a child or more remote descendant by adoption shall be disregarded.

　　　　(d)　　Subparagraphs (a) (2), (3) and (6) and paragraph (b) of this Section shall be deemed to be declaratory of the law prevailing in this State at the effective date of this Act.

¶ 195.　*Trusts*

　　§ 5.　　**Trusts.**　(a) Subject to the provisions of paragraphs (e) and (f) of this Section, a trust containing any limitation which, but for this paragraph (a), would violate the rule against perpetuities (as modified by Section 4) shall terminate at the expiration of a period of (A) 21 years after the death of the last to die of all of the beneficiaries of the instrument who were living at the date when the period of the rule against perpetuities commenced to run or (B) 21 years after that date if no beneficiary of the instrument was then living, unless events occur which cause an earlier termination in accordance with the terms of the instrument and then the principal shall be distributed as provided by the instrument.

　　　　(b)　　Subject to the provisions of paragraphs (c), (d) and (e) of this Section, when a trust terminates because of the application of paragraph (a) of this Section, the trustee shall distribute the principal to those persons who would be the heirs at law of the maker of the instrument if he died at the expiration of the period specified in paragraph (a) of this Section and in the proportions then specified by statute, unless the trust was created by the exercise of a power of appointment and then the principal shall be distributed to the person who would have received it if the power had not been exercised.

(c)   Before any distribution of principal is made pursuant to paragraph (b) of this Section, the trustee shall distribute, out of principal, to each living beneficiary who, but for termination of the trust because of the application of paragraph (a) of this Section, would have been entitled to be paid income after the expiration of the period specified in paragraph (a) of this Section, an amount equal to the present value (determined as provided in paragraph (d) of this Section) of the income which the beneficiary would have been entitled to be paid after the expiration of that period.

(d)   [Omitted]

(e)   [Omitted]

(f)   [Omitted]

2.   Chapter 76

¶ 1.   *Joint tenancy defined—Presumption of tenancy in common—Survivorship rights*

§ 1. No estate in joint tenancy in any lands, tenements or hereditaments, or in any parts thereof or interest therein, shall be held or claimed under any grant, legacy or conveyance whatsoever heretofore or hereafter made, other than to executors and trustees, unless the premises therein mentioned shall expressly be thereby declared to pass not in tenancy in common but in joint tenancy; and every such estate other than to executors and trustees (unless otherwise expressly declared as aforesaid, or unless, as to a devise or conveyance of homestead property, expressly declared to pass to a husband and wife as tenants by the entirety in the manner provided by Section 1c), shall be deemed to be in tenancy in common and all conveyances heretofore made, or which hereafter may be made, wherein the premises therein mentioned were or shall be expressly declared to pass not in tenancy in common but in joint tenancy, are hereby declared to have created an estate in joint tenancy with the accompanying right of survivorship the same as it existed prior to the passage of "An Act to amend Section 1 of an Act entitled: 'An Act to revise the law in relation to joint rights and obligations,' approved February 25, 1874, in force July 1, 1874," approved June 26, 1917.

C.   MINNESOTA

§ 500.02.   *Estates of inheritance*

Every estate of inheritance shall continue to be termed a fee simple, or fee; and every such estate, when not defeasible or conditional, shall be a fee simple absolute or an absolute fee.

§ 500.03.   *Effect of conveyance to grantee in fee tail*

In all cases where any person, if this chapter had not been passed, would at any time hereafter become seized in fee tail of any lands, tenements, or hereditaments by virtue of any devise, gift, grant, or other conveyance heretofore made, or hereafter to be made, or by any other means, such person, instead of becoming seized thereof in fee tail, shall be deemed and adjudged to be seized thereof as in fee simple.

§ 500.04.   *Conveyance by owner of fee tail estate*

Where lands, tenements, or hereditaments heretofore have been devised, granted, or otherwise conveyed by a tenant in tail, and the person to whom such devise, grant, or other conveyance has been made, or that person's heirs or assigns, have from the time such devise took effect, or from the time such grant or conveyance was made, to the day of passing this chapter, been in the uninterrupted possession of such lands, tenements, or hereditaments, and claiming and holding the same under or by virtue of such devise, grant, or other conveyance, they shall be deemed as good and legal to all intents and purposes as if such tenant in tail had, at the time of making such devise, grant, or other conveyance, been seized in fee simple of such lands, tenements, or hereditaments, any law to the contrary notwithstanding.

§ 500.14. *Future estates; construction, validity, and effect of creating instruments*

Subdivision 1.   Failure of heirs or issue.   Unless a different intent is effectively manifested, whenever property is limited upon the death of any person without "heirs" or "heirs of the body" or "issue" general or special, or "descendants" or "offspring" or "children" or any such relative described by other terms, the limitation is to take effect only when that person dies not having such relative living at the time of the person's death, or in gestation and born alive thereafter, and is not a limitation to take effect upon the indefinite failure of such relatives; nor, unless a different intent is effectively manifested, does the limitation mean that death without such relative is restricted in time to the lifetime of the creator of the interest.

Subdivision 2.   Alternative future estates.   Two or more future estates may also be created, to take effect in the alternative, so that if the first in order fails to vest the next in succession shall be substituted for it, and take effect accordingly.

Subdivision 3.   Probability of contingency.   No future estate, otherwise valid, shall be void on the ground of the probability or improbability of the contingency on which it is limited to take effect.

Subdivision 4.   Certain remainders vest by purchase.   When a remainder is limited to the heirs, or heirs of the body, of a person to whom a life estate in the same premises is given, the persons who, on the termination of the life estate, are the heirs or heirs of the body of such tenant for life shall be entitled to take as purchasers, by virtue of the remainder so limited to them. No conveyance, transfer, devise, or bequest of an interest, legal or equitable, in real or personal property, shall fail to take effect by purchase because limited to a person or persons, howsoever described, who would take the same interest by descent or distribution.

Subdivision 5. Posthumous children as remainderpersons.   When a future estate is limited to heirs, or issue, or children, posthumous children shall be entitled to take in the same manner as if living at the death of their parent.

Subdivision 6. Effect of posthumous birth on event of "death without issue." A future estate, depending on the contingency of the death of any person without heirs or issue or children, shall be defeated by the birth of a posthumous child of such person capable of taking by descent.

§ 500.15. *Future estates; protection from destructibility rules*

Subdivision 1. Destruction of precedent estate by act of its owner. No expectant estate can be defeated or barred by any alienation or other act of the owner of the intermediate or precedent estate, nor by any destruction of such precedent estate, by disseizin, forfeiture, surrender, merger, or otherwise.

Subdivision 2. Exception. Subdivision 1 shall not be construed to prevent an expectant estate from being defeated in any manner, or by any act or means, which the party creating such estate has, in the creation thereof, provided or authorized; nor shall an expectant estate thus liable to be defeated be on that ground adjudged void in its creation.

Subdivision 3. Premature determination of precedent estate. No remainder, valid in its creation, shall be defeated by the determination of the precedent estate before the happening of the contingency on which the remainder is limited to take effect; but, should such contingency afterward happen, the remainder shall take effect in the same manner and to the same extent as if the precedent estate had continued to the same period.

§ 500.19. *Division*

Subdivision 1. According to number. Estates, in respect to the number and connection of their owners, are divided into estates in severalty, in joint tenancy, and in common; the nature and properties of which, respectively, shall continue to be such as are now established by law, except so far as the same may be modified by the provisions of this chapter.

Subdivision 2. Construction of grants and devises. All grants and devises of lands, made to two or more persons, shall be construed to create estates in common, and not in joint tenancy, unless expressly declared to be in joint tenancy. This section shall not apply to mortgages, nor to devises or grants made in trust, or to executors.

Subdivision 3. Joint tenancy requirements abolished. The common law requirement for unity of time, title, interest, and possession in the creation of a joint tenancy is abolished.

Subdivision 4. Converting estates. [Omitted]

Subdivision 5. Severance of estates in joint tenancy. [Omitted]

§ 500.20.   *Defeasible estates*

Subdivision 1. Normal conditions and limitations. When any covenants, conditions, restrictions or extensions thereof annexed to a grant, devise or conveyance of land are, or shall become, merely nominal, and of no actual and substantial benefit to the party or parties to whom or in whose favor they are to be performed, they may be wholly disregarded; and a failure to perform the same shall in no case operate as a basis of forfeiture of the lands subject thereto.

Subdivision 2a. Restriction of duration of condition. Except for any right to reenter or to repossess as provided in subdivision 3, all private covenants, conditions, or restrictions created by which the title or use of real property is affected, cease to be valid and operative 30 years after the date of the deed, or other instrument, or the date of the probate of the will, creating them, and may be disregarded.

This subdivision does not apply to covenants, conditions or restrictions:

(1)   that were created before August 1, 1988, by deed or other instrument dated on or after August 1, 1982, or by will the date of death of the testator of which was on or after August 1, 1982;

(2)   [Omitted];

(3)   [Omitted];

(4)   [Omitted];

(5)   [Omitted];

(6)   [Omitted];

(7)   [Omitted].

Subdivision 3. Time to assert power of termination. Hereafter any right to reenter or to repossess land on account of breach made in a condition subsequent shall be barred unless such right is asserted by entry or action within six years after the happening of the breach upon which such right is predicated.

D.   NEW MEXICO

1.   Chapter 42

§ 42-9-4.   *[Filing complaint or statement, affidavit and bond; issuance of writ; property subject to attachment.]*

A creditor wishing to sue his debtor by attachment, may place in the clerk's office of the district court of any county in this state, having jurisdiction, a complaint, or other lawful statement of his cause of action, and shall also file an affidavit and bond; and thereupon such creditor may sue out an original attachment against the lands, tenements, goods, moneys, effects, credits and any right, title, lien or interest whether legal or equitable upon, in or to real or personal, tangible or intangible property whether present or possessory or reversionary or in remainder and all property which could be reached upon execution or upon equitable proceedings in aid of execution, of the debtor in whosesoever hands they may be except such property as is now, or may hereafter be, specifically exempted from attachment or execution by law and except interests of beneficiaries in spendthrift trusts for whom spendthrift trusts are or may be created.

2.   Chapter 45

§ 45-1-201.   *General Definitions.*

A.   As used in the Probate Code, and unless the context otherwise requires:

....

(9)   "estate" means the property of the decedent, trust or other person whose affairs are subject to the Probate Code as originally constituted and as it exists from time to time during administration;

....

(31) "property" includes both real and personal property or any interest therein and means anything that may be the subject of ownership;

....

§ 45-2-101. *Intestate estate.*

Any part of the estate of a decedent not effectively disposed of by his will passes to his heirs as prescribed in Sections 2-101 through 2-113 [45-2-101 to 45-2-113 NMSA 1978] of the Probate Code.

§ 45-2-1001. *Statutory rule against perpetuities.*

A.   A nonvested property interest is invalid unless:

(1)   when the interest is created, it is certain to vest or terminate no later than twenty-one years after the death of an individual then alive; or

(2)   the interest either vests or terminates within ninety years after its creation.

B.   [Omitted].

C.   [Omitted].

D.   In determining whether a nonvested property interest or a power of appointment is valid under each Paragraph (1) of Subsections A, B and C of this section, the possibility that a child will be born to an individual after the individual's death shall be disregarded.

E.   If, in measuring a period from the creation of a trust or other property arrangement, language in a governing instrument seeks to postpone the vesting or termination of any interest or trust until, seeks to disallow the vesting or termination of any interest or trust beyond, seeks to require all interests or trusts to vest or terminate no later than, or seeks to operate in effect in any similar fashion upon the later of:

(1)   the expiration of a period of time not exceeding twenty-one years after the death of the survivor of specified lives in being at the creation of the trust or other property arrangement; or

(2)   the expiration of a period of time that exceeds or might exceed twenty-one years after the death of the survivor of lives in being at the creation of the trust or other property arrangement, then the portion of the language described in Paragraph (2) above is inoperative if and to the extent it produces a period of time that exceeds twenty-one years after the death of the survivor of the lives specified in Paragraph (1) above.

§ 45-2-1003. *Reformation.*

Upon the petition of an interested person, a court shall reform a disposition in the manner that most closely approximates the transferor's manifested plan of distribution and is within the ninety years allowed by each Paragraph (2) of Subsections A, B or C of Section 45-2-1001 NMSA 1978 if:

A.   a nonvested property interest or a power of appointment becomes invalid under Section 45-2-1001 NMSA 1978;

B.   a class gift is not but might become invalid under Section 45-2-1001 NMSA 1978 and the time has arrived when the share of any class member is to take effect in possession or enjoyment; or

C.   a nonvested property interest that is not validated by Paragraph (1) of Subsection A of Section 45-2-1001 NMSA 1978 can vest but not within ninety years after its creation.

§ 45-2-1004. *Exclusions.*

Section 45-2-1001 NMSA 1978 does not apply to:

A.   a nonvested property interest or a power of appointment arising out of a nondonative transfer, except a nonvested property interest or a power of appointment arising out of:

(1)   a premarital or postmarital agreement;

(2)   a separation or divorce settlement;

(3)   a spouse's election;

(4)   a similar arrangement arising out of a prospective, existing or pervious marital relationship between the parties;

(5)   a contract to make or not to revoke a will or trust;

(6)   a contract to exercise or not to exercise a power of appointment;

(7)   a transfer in satisfaction of a duty of support; or

(8)   a reciprocal transfer;

B.   a fiduciary's power relating to the administration or management of assets, including the power of a fiduciary to sell, lease or mortgage property and the power of a fiduciary to determine principal and income;

C.   a power to appoint a fiduciary;

D.   a discretionary power of a trustee to distribute principal before termination of a trust to a beneficiary having an indefeasibly vested interest in the income and principal;

E.   a nonvested property interest held by a charity, government or governmental agency or subdivision if the nonvested property interest is preceded by an interest held by another charity, government or governmental agency or subdivision;

F.   a nonvested property interest in or a power of appointment with respect to a trust or other property arrangement forming part of a pension, profit-sharing, stock bonus, health, disability, death benefit, income deferral or other current or deferred benefit plan for one or more employees, independent contractors or their beneficiaries or spouses, to which contributions are made for the purpose of distributing to or for the benefit of the participants or their beneficiaries or spouses the property, income or principal in the trust or other property arrangement, except a nonvested property interest or a power of appointment that is created by an election of a participant or a beneficiary or spouse; or

G.   a property interest, power of appointment or arrangement that was not subject to the common-law rule against perpetuities or that is excluded by another statute of New Mexico.

§ 45-2-1005. *Prospective application.*

A.   Except as extended by Subsection B of this section, Sections 45-2-1001 through 45-2-1005 NMSA 1978 apply to a nonvested property interest or a power of appointment that is created on or after July 1, 1992. For purposes of this section, a nonvested property interest or a power of appointment created by the exercise of a power of appointment is created when the power is irrevocably exercised or when a revocable exercise becomes irrevocable.

B.   If a nonvested property interest or a power of appointment was created before July 1, 1992 and is determined in a judicial proceeding, commenced on or after July 1, 1992, to violate the New Mexico rule against perpetuities as that rule existed before July 1, 1992, a court, upon the petition of an interested person, may reform the disposition in the manner that most closely approximates the transferor's manifested plan of distribution and is within the limits of the rule against perpetuities applicable when the nonvested property interest or power of appointment was created.

§ 45-2-1006. *Supervision.*

Sections 45-2-1001 through 45-2-1005 NMSA 1978 supersede the rule of the common law known as the rule against perpetuities.

3.　　Chapter 47

§ 47-1-2.　*Monopolies; entailments; primogeniture.*

Monopolies are contrary to the genius of a free government and shall never be allowed, nor shall the law of primogeniture or entailments ever be in force in this state.

§ 47-1-4.　*[Conveyances authorized.]*

Any person or persons, or body politic, holding, or who may hold, any right or title to real estate in this state, be it absolute or limited, in possession, remainder or reversion, may convey the same in the manner and subject to the restrictions prescribed in this chapter.

§ 47-1-15.　*[Joint grantees or devisees; tenancy in common.]*

All interest in any real estate, either granted or bequeathed to two or more persons other than executors or trustees, shall be held in common, unless it be clearly expressed in said grant or bequest that it shall be held by both parties.

§ 47-1-16.　*[Instrument of conveyance; prima facie evidence of joint tenancy.]*

An instrument conveying or transferring title to real or personal property to two or more persons as joint tenants, to two or more persons and to the survivors of them and the heirs and assigns of the survivor, or to two or more persons with right of survivorship, shall be prima facie evidence that such property is held in a joint tenancy and shall be conclusive as to purchasers or encumbrancers for value. In any litigation involving the issue of such tenancy a preponderance of the evidence shall be sufficient to establish the same.

§ 47-1-17.　*[Entailed estates.]*

Whenever a conveyance or bequest is made wherein the conveyor or testator shall hold possession of property, be it lands or tenements, in law or equity, as under English Statute of Edward the First, styled the entail statute,[*] and said property is to be perpetuated in the family, each one of said conveyances or bequests shall only invest the conveyors or testators[**] with possession during their lifetime, who shall possess and hold the right and title to said premises, and no others the same as a tenant for life is recognized by law; and at the death of said conveyor or testator said lands and tenements shall descend to the children of said conveyor or testator, to be equally divided among them as absolute tenants in common; and if there should be but one child, it shall descend absolutely to it; and if any child should die, the part which he or she should have received shall be given to his or her successor, and if there should be no such successor, then it shall descend to his or her legal heirs.

§ 47-1-18. *[Reversion; "heirs" and "successors" defined.]*

When a balance or residue, in lands or tenements, goods or property, is limited by writing or otherwise to take effect after the decease of any person without heirs, or bodily heirs or succession, the words heirs and successors shall be so construed as to mean heirs or successors living, at the time of the decease of the person styled ancestor.

§ 47-1-19. *[Rights of heirs of life tenant when made remaindermen.]*

When the remainder of a possession is limited to the heirs or heirs of the body of a person who holds said property as a life estate, in these premises the persons who at the termination of said life estate, are to be heirs or heirs of the body of said life estate, shall be authorized to purchase the same [take as purchasers] by virtue of the remainder of the possession so limited in them.

---

[*]This somewhat off-hand reference is to the enactment of Parliament known more commonly as De Donis Conditionalibus, 13 Edw. I, ch. 1 (1285), given short shrift by the discussion above. De Donis, as it is known by intimates, granted recognition to the fee tail as you have mastered it and protected the rights of the lineal heirs from disentailment.

[**]This reference quite obviously should be to conveyees and legatees.

§ 47-1-20. *[Remainder to unborn child.]*

When any possession has been or shall be conveyed limiting the remainder of the possession to the son or. daughter of any person, born after the death of its parent, possession shall be taken the same as if he or she was born during the life of the parent, although no possession should have been conveyed to sustain the remainder of a contingent possession after his death, and after this an absolute possession or bequest may be made, commencing in the future, in writing in the same manner as by will.

§ 47-1-21. *[Future possession dependent on death without heirs; effect of birth of posthumous child.]*

A future possession depending upon the contingency of the death of a person without heirs shall be revoked by the birth of a posthumous son or daughter of said person capable of succeeding him.

§ 47-1-23. *[Transfer of reversion authorized.]*

That the possibility or right of reversion for breach or violation of condition or conditions subsequent contained in any deed or other instrument conveying real estate in the state of New Mexico, is hereby made assignable, and the grantor in any such instrument heretofore or hereafter made affecting real estate in the state of New Mexico, is given the right to assign and transfer such future contingent right of reentry, forfeiture and reversion for violation or breach of such condition or conditions subsequent.

§ 47-1-24. *[Rights of transferee of reversion.]*

The assignee of or any successor to the right of reentry, forfeiture and reversion for breach or violation of condition or conditions subsequent, is hereby given upon such assignment, all of the rights and privileges of the original grantor for the enforcement of reentry, forfeiture and reversion when any such condition or conditions subsequent shall have been breached or broken, including all legal and equitable remedies for the judicial enforcement of such right or rights.

§ 47-1-33. *[Unnecessary terms; construction of deeds or reservations.]*

In a conveyance or reservation of real estate the terms, "heirs," "assigns" or other technical words of inheritance shall not be necessary to convey or reserve an estate in fee. A deed or reservation of real estate shall be construed to convey or reserve an estate in fee simple, unless a different intention clearly appears in the deed.

§ 47-1-35. *[Conveyance or mortgage to joint tenants.]*

In a conveyance or mortgage of real estate, the designation of two or more grantees "as joint tenants" shall be construed to mean that the conveyance is to the grantees as joint tenants, and not as tenants in common, and to the survivor of them and the heirs and assigns of the survivor.

§ 47-1-36. *Joint tenancies defined; creation.*

A joint tenancy in real property is one owned by two or more persons, each owning the whole and an equal undivided share, by a title created by a single devise or conveyance, when expressly declared in the will or conveyance to be a joint tenancy, or by conveyance from a sole owner to himself and others, or from tenants in common to themselves, or to themselves and others, or from husband and wife when holding as community property or otherwise to themselves or to themselves and others, when expressly declared in the conveyance to be a joint tenancy, or when granted or devised to executors or trustees.

E.   NORTH DAKOTA

1.   Title 30.1

§ 30.1-04-01 (2-101).[*]   *Intestate estate.*

Any part of the estate of a decedent not effectively disposed of by his will passes to his heirs as prescribed in the following sections of this title.

§ 30.1-04-02 (2-102).   *Share of the spouse.*

The intestate share of the surviving spouse is:

1.   If there is no surviving issue or parent of the decedent, the entire intestate estate.

2.   If there is no surviving issue but the decedent is survived by a parent or parents, the first fifty thousand dollars, plus one-half of the balance of the intestate estate.

3.   If there are surviving issue all of whom are issue of the surviving spouse also, the first fifty thousand dollars, plus one-half of the balance of the intestate estate.

4.   If there are surviving issue, one or more of whom are not issue of the surviving spouse, one-half of the intestate estate.

§ 30.1-04-03 (2-103).   *Share of heirs other than surviving spouse.*

The part of the intestate estate not passing to the surviving spouse under section 30.1-04-02, or the entire intestate estate if there is no surviving spouse, passes as follows:

---

[*]The parenthetical references are to the corresponding Uniform Probate Code sections.

1. To the issue of the decedent. If they are all of the same degree of kinship to the decedent they take equally, but if of unequal degree, then those of more remote degree take by representation.

2. If there is no surviving issue, to his parent or parents equally.

3. If there is no surviving issue or parent, to the issue of the parents or either of them by representation.

4. If there is no surviving issue, parent, or issue of a parent, but the decedent is survived by one or more grandparents or issue of grandparents, half of the estate passes to the paternal grandparents if both survive, or to the surviving paternal grandparent, or to the issue of the paternal grandparents if both are deceased, by representation; and the other half passes to the maternal relatives in the same manner. If there be no surviving grandparent or issue of grandparent on either the paternal or the maternal side, the entire estate passes to the relatives on the other side in the same manner as the half.[*]

§ 30.1-04-03.1. *Persons related to decedent through two lines.*

A person related to the decedent through two lines of relationship is entitled to only a single share based on the relationship that would entitle him to the larger share.

§ 30.1-04-04 (2-104). *Requirement that heir survive decedent for one hundred twenty hours.*

Any person who fails to survive the decedent by one hundred twenty hours is deemed to have predeceased the decedent for purposes of homestead allowance, exempt property, and intestate succession, and the decedent's heirs are determined accordingly. If the time of death of the decedent or of the person who would otherwise be an heir, or the times of death of both, cannot be determined, and it

---

[*]You will note that this section and the preceding one define the "heirs" differently than did the common law in a number of respects: the spouse is a potential heir, male domination is gone and the class of heirs is more limited, reaching only as far as issue of grandparents.

cannot be established that the person who would otherwise be an heir has survived the decedent by one hundred twenty hours, it is deemed that the person failed to survive for the required period. This section is not to be applied where its application would result in a taking of intestate estate by the state under section 30.1-04-05.

§ 30.1-04-05 (2-105). *No taker.*

If there is no taker under the provisions of this title, the intestate estate passes to the state for the support of the common schools and an action for the recovery of such property and to reduce it into the possession of the state or for its sale and conveyance may be brought by the attorney general or by the state's attorney in the district court of the county in which the property is situated.[*]

§ 30.1-04-06 (2-106). *Representation.*

If representation is called for by this title, the estate is divided into as many shares as there are surviving heirs in the nearest degree of kinship and deceased persons in the same degree who left issue who survive the decedent, each surviving heir in the nearest degree receiving one share and the share of each deceased person in the same degree being divided among his issue in the same manner.

§ 30.1-04-07 (2-107). *Kindred of half blood.*

Relatives of the half blood inherit the same share they would inherit if they were of the whole blood.

---

[*]The common law equivalent of this statute was the doctrine of escheat. Under the common law, the definition of "heir" was broad enough that ordinarily every decedent had an heir. Compare § 30.1-04-02, 03 above. Of course, practically speaking, it was/is often difficult to identify a remote collateral heir.

§ 30.1-04-08 (2-108). *Afterborn heirs.*

Relatives of the decedent conceived before his death but born thereafter inherit as if they had been born in the lifetime of the decedent.

§ 30.1-04-09 (2-109). *Meaning of child and related terms.*

If, for purposes of intestate succession, a relationship of parent and child must be established to determine succession by, through, or from a person:

1.   An adopted person is the child of an adopting parent and not of the natural parents, except that adoption of a child by the spouse of a natural parent has no effect on the relationship between the child and either natural parent.

2.   In cases not covered by subsection 1, a person is the child of its parents regardless of the marital status of its parents and the parent and child relationship may be established under the Uniform Parentage Act.

§ 30.1-04-10 (2-110). *Advancements.*

If a person dies intestate as to all his estate, property which he gave in his lifetime to an heir is treated as an advancement against the latter's share of the estate only if declared in a contemporaneous writing by the decedent or acknowledged in writing by the heir to be an advancement. For this purpose the property advanced is valued as of the time the heir came into possession or enjoyment of the property or as of the time of death of the decedent, whichever first occurs. If the recipient of the property fails to survive the decedent, the property is not taken into account in computing the intestate share to be received by the recipient's issue, unless the declaration or acknowledgment provides otherwise.

§ 30.1-04-11 (2-111). *Debts to decedent.*

A debt owed to the decedent is not charged against the intestate share of any person except the debtor. If the debtor fails to survive the decedent, the debt is not taken into account in computing the intestate share of the debtor's issue.

§ 30.1-04-12 (2-112). *Alienage.*

No person is disqualified to take as an heir because he or a person through whom he claims is or has been an alien.

§ 30.1-04-13 (2-113). *Dower and curtesy abolished.*

The estates of dower and curtesy are abolished.[*]

2.   Title 47

§ 47-02-08. *"Interest in common" defined.*

An interest in common is one owned by several persons not in joint ownership or partnership. Every interest created in favor of several persons in their own right is an interest in common, unless acquired by them in partnership for partnership purposes, or unless declared in its creation to be a joint tenancy.

§ 47-02-10. *"Present interest" defined.*

A present interest means that the owner is entitled to the immediate possession of the property.

---

[*]These common law estates, created by law in a widow upon the death of her husband and in a man upon marriage were not within the scope of this book. However, they provide examples of life estates at common law. *See* 2 R. Powell, *The Law of Real Property* ¶¶ 209-213 (P. Rohan, rev. ed. 1991).

---

§ 47-02-15. *Future estates—Classification.*

A future interest is either vested or contingent. It is vested when there is a person in being who would have a right, defeasible or indefeasible, to the immediate possession of the property upon the ceasing of the intermediate or precedent interest. It is contingent while the person in whom or the event upon which it is limited to take effect remains uncertain.

§ 47-02-16. *Alternative contingencies.*

Two or more future interests may be created to take effect in the alternative so that if the first in order fails to vest, the next in succession shall be substituted for it and take effect accordingly.

§ 47-02-18. *Future interests pass.*

Future interests pass by succession, will, and transfer in the same manner as present interests.

§ 47-02-20. *Mere possibility not an interest.*

A mere possibility, such as the expectancy of an heir apparent, is not to be deemed an interest of any kind.

§ 47-02-24. *Illegal conditions void.*

If a condition precedent requires the performance of an act wrong in itself, the instrument containing it is so far void, and the right cannot exist. If it requires the performance of an act not wrong of itself, but otherwise unlawful, the instrument takes effect and the condition is void.

§ 47-02-25. *Restraints upon marriage void—Use until marriage.*

Conditions imposing restraints upon marriage, except upon the marriage of a minor, or of the widow of the person by whom the condition is imposed, are void. This does not affect limitations when the intent was not to forbid marriage but only to give the use until marriage.

§ 47-02-26. *Restraints on alienation—When void.*

Conditions restraining alienation, when repugnant to the interest created, are void.

§ 47-02-30. *Future interest—Effect of change of intermediate interest.*

No future interest can be defeated or barred by any alienation or other act of the owner of the intermediate or precedent interest, nor by any destruction of such precedent interest by forfeiture, surrender, merger, or otherwise, except as provided by section 47-02-32, or when a forfeiture is imposed by statute as a penalty for the violation thereof.

§ 47-02-32. *Future interest—Effect of determination of precedent interest— Contingent remainders not artificially destructible.*

No future interest, valid in its creation, is defeated by the determination of the precedent interest before the happening of the contingency on which the future interest is limited to take effect, but should such contingency afterwards happen, the future interest takes effect in the same manner and to the same extent as if the precedent interest had continued to the same period.

§ 47-02-33. *Rights of owner of life estate.*

The owner of a life estate may use the land in the same manner as the owner of a fee simple, except that he must do no act to the injury of the inheritance.

§ 47-04-04. *"Estate in fee" defined.*

Every estate of inheritance is a fee, and every such estate, when not defeasible or conditional, is a fee simple or an absolute fee.

§ 47-04-05. *Estates tail abolished—Declared fees.*

Estates tail are abolished and every estate which would be adjudged a fee tail at common law is a fee simple, and if no valid remainder is limited thereon, is a fee simple absolute.

§ 47-04-06. *Fee tail valid as contingent limitation upon a fee.*

Where a remainder in fee is limited upon any estate which, by the common law, would be adjudged a fee tail, such remainder is valid as a contingent limitation upon a fee and vests in possession on the death of the first taker, without issue living at the time of his death.

§ 47-04-07. *Estate for life is freehold.*

An estate during the life of a third person, whether limited to heirs or otherwise, is a freehold.

§ 47-04-09. *"Reversion" defined.*

A reversion is the residue of an estate left by operation of law in the grantor or his successors or in the successors of a testator commencing in possession on the determination of a particular estate granted or devised.

§ 47-04-10. *"Remainder" defined.*

When a future estate, other than a reversion, is dependent on a precedent estate, it may be called a remainder and may be created and transferred by that name.

§ 47-04-20. *Remainder limited to heirs of body of life tenant—Rule in Shelley's Case abolished.*

When a remainder is limited to the heirs, or heirs of the body, of a person to whom a life estate in the same property is given, the persons who, on the termination of the life estate are the successors or heirs of the body of the owner for life, are entitled to take by virtue of the remainder so limited to them and not as mere successors of the owner for life.

§ 47-04-21. *Remainder limited on estate for life or years—When effective.*

When a remainder on an estate for life or for years is not limited on a contingency defeating or avoiding such precedent estate, it shall be deemed intended to take effect only on the death of the first taker or the expiration by lapse of time of such term of years.

§ 47-09-14. *"Without issue" defined.*

When a future interest is limited by a grant to take effect on the death of any person without heirs, or heirs of his body, without issue, or in equivalent words, such words must be taken to mean successors or issue living at the death of the person named as ancestor.

§ 47-09-15. *Words of inheritance or succession unnecessary to fee.*

Words of inheritance or succession shall not be requisite to transfer a fee in real property.

§ 47-10-13. *Grant presumes fee simple title.*

A fee simple title is presumed to be intended to pass by a grant of real property unless it appears from the grant that a lesser estate was intended.

§ 47-10-16. *Reconveyance when estate defeated by non–performance of condition subsequent.*

When a grant is made upon condition subsequent and subsequently is defeated by the nonperformance of the condition, the person otherwise entitled to hold under the grant must reconvey the property to the grantor or his successors by grant duly acknowledged for record.